Black BROADWAY
IN WASHINGTON, D.C.

Black BROADWAY
IN WASHINGTON, D.C.

BRIANA A. THOMAS

Foreword by Congresswoman Eleanor Holmes Norton

THE
History
PRESS

Published by The History Press
Charleston, SC
www.historypress.com

First published 2021

Manufactured in the United States

ISBN 9781467139298

Library of Congress Control Number: 2020944234

Notice: The information in this book is true and complete to the best of our knowledge. It is offered without guarantee on the part of the author or The History Press. The author and The History Press disclaim all liability in connection with the use of this book.

This book is dedicated, with love, to my grandmother Evelyn Thomas. Thank you for sharing your precious U Street memories with me.

CONTENTS

FOREWORD

When I was a girl growing up in segregated Washington, U Street was more than a street or a place or even a neighborhood. It was all of those and much more. U Street was more than the Black business district or the Black entertainment district for which it is best remembered. U Street was the self-created, self-contained Black hub of our city. The District was segregated by the United States Congress. Many of the institutions that defined African Americans in the District revolved around this centrally located section of the city. The U Street district was home to the District's oldest churches; like Vermont Avenue Baptist; legitimate theaters, like the Howard Theatre, restaurants; nightclubs; and other entertainments open to all, in defiance of segregated downtown for whites only.

Although U Street itself is only a mile long, and home to only a small fraction of public accommodations in the city, the rest of the District was largely closed to African Americans, except for the central library on downtown K Street. Blacks could not buy or rent homes in the District, except in neighborhoods being abandoned by whites who took flight as the first Blacks moved in. African American luminaries fared no better, from musical great Duke Ellington to Dr. Charles Drew of Howard University Medical School, developer of the first blood bank, whose daughters went to public school with me. Yet fencing in Black people where they lived and went to school did not have the effect one might expect.

These artificial barriers invited African Americans to learn how to succeed in America while still confined within a closed society. Seeking one's fortune within a society of denial led to a focus on education. Howard University, Miner Teachers College and the acclaimed Dunbar High School, where I went to high school, were all located close to U Street. These African American educational institutions were cherished as the only vehicles available to move up in a society characterized by barriers instead of opportunity. The African American focus on education showed an understanding of what was necessary to find decent work in the local white-collar economy, whose chief industry was and remains the federal agencies. For most work, even in the lowest ranks of federal employment, at least a high school education was required—and more to move up.

White people have been the majority in the District for most of its 229 years. Although part of the same economy, whites in the city had no similar history of prizing education, perhaps because of opportunities available in the wider private economy in the trades and in business in nearby Maryland and Virginia, where racial segregation was also legally required. Blacks were left to wonder how whites, who seemed not to put the same priority on education, could possibly think themselves superior to Blacks, who aspired to high standards in education. Dunbar High School, the only college preparatory Black high school in the District, for example, gained a reputation that enabled Dunbar graduates to attend the best colleges in the country. Dunbar was known for many notable graduates in the twentieth century, among them Senator Edward Brooke; Robert Weaver, the first African American Housing and Urban Development secretary; and Wesley Brown, the first African American to graduate from the U.S. Naval Academy.

The strong education tradition in the District's African American community had much to do with the refusal to accept the inferiority assigned to them by the larger society, particularly in the South, where the District is located. In the District of Columbia, it was possible to live in a contained African American society. Further down south, public transportation compelled Black people to participate in their own unequal treatment by riding in the least preferred seats. No such daily indignity was forced on African Americans in the nation's capital. The segregation that guaranteed limited contact with whites left Blacks in the District outside of the daily and immediate psychology of inferiority.

The African American community itself managed to provide protective insulation from the notion that segregation equaled inferiority. The District left me well prepared to go away to college and to law school, to participate in the Student Nonviolent Coordinating Committee and to begin a life of working against segregation and for equality. Sheltered from feelings of inferiority by our African American community, fueled by a focus on education and embraced by our own segregated community centered on U Street, everything seemed possible.

—Eleanor Holmes Norton,
congresswoman for Washington, D.C.

ACKNOWLEDGEMENTS

This book began as an editorial fellowship assignment at *Washingtonian Magazine* and gradually expanded into an in-depth look at the U Street neighborhood located in Washington's northwest quadrant. I'm grateful for all of the advisers, researchers, teachers, historians, students and community members who assisted me in telling the one-of-a kind Black history of the corridor.

A special thanks to Dr. Bernard Demczuk, who I met a decade ago at Ben's Chili Bowl as a participant in one of his walking history tours around the neighborhood. Dr. Demczuk has graciously shared his knowledge of Washington with me and has encouraged me to discover the story of this community one chapter of my book at a time.

I'd also like to thank the Lee family at Lee's Flower and Card Shop; in particular, Richard Lee and his daughter Stacie Lee Banks. Both Richard and Stacie were so welcoming when I began my project in 2016, and whether it was providing their personal narratives, references, photographs or just sound advice, they made a huge impact on my work, and their kindness will always be remembered.

To the editors at *Washingtonian Magazine*, thank you. I was a young fellow just beginning my journalism journey when articles editor Kristen Hinman asked me if I wanted to compile a photo-story essay showing U Street during the golden years of Black Broadway. I said yes, and well, the rest is history. Editor Michael Schaffer has been a great coach since the early stages of my research, and all of his thought-provoking questions and guidance are greatly appreciated.

ACKNOWLEDGEMENTS

Much gratitude to the families of U Street: The Alis at Ben's Chili Bowl, the Mitchells at Industrial Bank, the Drew-Jarvis family, Eddie at JC Lofton Tailors and many others whose vibrant memories helped shape this book.

I'm so thankful to Congresswoman Eleanor Holmes Norton for all of her contributions to the city of Washington. It's an honor to have her as a contributor to my book. Representative Norton authored a power-packed foreword!

Thank you to Jessica Smith at the Historical Society of Washington for sifting through documents for me on several different occasions over the years.

The Prints and Photographs Division at the Library of Congress, in particular reference specialist Kristi Finefield, worked with speed and efficiency to help me in my digging for images and artifacts. I owe this department a great debt of gratitude for my time-capturing cover image!

To the professors and faculty who I interviewed at Howard University, as well as the librarians who either located sources for me or pointed me in the appropriate direction, thank you.

I met Brianna Rhodes during my graduate studies at the University of Maryland College Park, and she has been a colleague and dear friend of mine ever since. Thank you for all of the late-night grammar checks and for single-handedly transcribing all of the interviews I used for my manuscript.

Kate Jenkins, my acquisitions editor at The History Press, has been so patient with me during this whole process, and for that I'm very thankful. I can still remember receiving my very first email from Kate asking me to submit a project proposal to The History Press. If it wasn't for your eye for talent and storytelling, I wouldn't have had the opportunity to write this book. You're awesome!

Much appreciation to all of the researchers and writers who explored U Street's story before I took on the task of working to preserve the area's history. A special thanks to Blair Ruble, Chris Myers Asch, C.R. Gibbs, Maurice Jackson and Derek Hyra, who have covered Washington's Black history with grace and detail. Your openness in sharing your research and findings with me is truly a demonstration of your characters and passion for keeping the African American voices of Washington alive.

The biggest thank-you goes to my family and friends who encouraged me, inspired me and most of all believed in me. It is because of their support and love that I was able to see this project through.

A BLOW TO SLAVERY EVERYWHERE

Marching through the nation's capital on the afternoon of April 19, 1866, were as many as five thousand African Americans overwhelmed with joy and pride. Cheering along the streets where slaves were once coffled, jailed and traded, a celebration of freedom had been long overdue.[1]

Four years before, 3,100 slaves[2] had been freed by President Abraham Lincoln's D.C. Emancipation Act, marking a day of triumph and, for many, a reflection of hardship.

With blue skies, a well-dressed procession, ten thousand Black spectators, music, flowers and banners reading "Lincoln the Liberator," the first annual District of Columbia Emancipation Day Parade commemorated the abolishment of slavery.[3]

But the years leading up to the end of bondage in Washington were far from celebratory. By 1800, slaves in Washington outnumbered freedpeople by five to one. Life for free and enslaved Blacks in the capital was very difficult, as one researcher noted, "Freedom was the first aim of every slave, even though life as a freedman might be harder than as a chattel bondsman."[4]

The nation's capital, established in 1791, was located on the Potomac River below a small port in Georgetown, a site chosen by President George Washington. Built at the expense of slave labor, the District of Columbia served as a new home for the federal government. The designated area for the capital was one hundred square miles, formed from land ceded by neighboring slaveholding states Maryland and Virginia. Maryland ceded

A sketch of the celebration of the abolition of slavery in the District of Columbia, April 19, 1866. *Library of Congress.*

sixty-nine square miles north of the Potomac River, while Virginia ceded the remaining lands to the south.[5]

Although no people of African descent owned land in Washington at the time, a Black man was chosen to assist in surveying the city. At the recommendation of Commissioner Andrew Ellicott of Baltimore, Benjamin Banneker, a self-taught scientist and astronomer assisted Major Pierre Charles L'Enfant in city planning. The president agreed to pay proprietors about sixty-seven dollars per acre for the land each owner sold to the country, and then he assigned L'Enfant with the task of constructing a layout for the newly purchased grounds.[6] The French engineer served under Washington in the Revolutionary War[7] with General Lafayette and had a personal friendship with Secretary of State Thomas Jefferson, a Virginian who was part of the congressional compromise enabling Washington to choose the exact site of the capital in the Residence Act of 1790.[8]

For five months, Banneker worked alongside L'Enfant, observing the city, dining next to white patrons and working to complete a map for the government buildings, streets and lots to come.[9] L'Enfant wrote to Washington on September 11, 1789, saying, "No nation had ever before

40

Congrefs of the United States:

AT THE SECOND SESSION,

Begun and held at the City of New-York on Monday the fourth
day of January, one thoufand feven hundred and ninety.

An ACT *for eftablifhing the Temporary and Permanent Seat of the Government
of the United States.*

BE it enacted by the SENATE *and* HOUSE *of* REPRESENTATIVES *of the United
States of America in Congrefs affembled,* That a diftrict of territory, not
exceeding ten miles fquare, to be located as hereafter directed on the river
Potomack, at fome place between the mouths of the Eaftern-Branch and Con-
nogochegue be, and the fame is hereby accepted for the permanent feat of the
government of the United States: *Provided neverthelefs,* That the operation of
the laws of the ftate within fuch diftrict fhall not be affected by this acceptance,
until the time fixed for the removal of the government thereto, and until
Congrefs fhall otherwife by law provide.

And be it further enacted, That the Prefident of the United States be authorized to appoint, and by fupplying vacancies happening from refufals to
act, or other caufes, to keep in appointment, as long as may be neceffary, three
commiffioners, who, or any two of whom, fhall under the direction of the
Prefident, furvey, and by proper metes and bounds, define and limit a diftrict
of territory, under the limitations above-mentioned ; and the diftrict fo defined,
limited and located, fhall be deemed the diftrict accepted by this act, for the
permanent feat of the government of the United States.

And be it enacted, That the faid commiffioners, or any two of them fhall
have power to purchafe or accept fuch quantity of land on the eaftern fide
of the faid river within the faid diftrict, as the Prefident fhall deem proper
for the ufe of the United States, and according to fuch plans as the Prefident
fhall approve, the faid commiffioners, or any two of them fhall, prior to the
firft Monday in December, in the year one thoufand eight hundred, provide
fuitable buildings for the accommodation of Congrefs, and of the Prefident,
and for the public offices of the government of the United States.

And be it enacted, That for defraying the expence of fuch purchafes and
buildings, the Prefident of the United States be authorized and requefted to
accept grants of money.

And be it enacted, That prior to the firft Monday in December next, all
offices attached to the feat of the government of the United States, fhall be
removed to, and until the faid firft Monday in December, in the year one
thoufand eight hundred, fhall remain at the city of Philadelphia, in the ftate
of Pennfylvania; at which place the feffion of Congrefs next enfuing the pre-
fent, fhall be held.

And be it enacted, That on the faid firft Monday in December, in the year
one thoufand eight hundred, the feat of the government of the United States,
fhall, by virtue of this act, be transferred to the diftrict and place aforefaid:
And all offices attached to the faid feat of government, fhall accordingly be
removed thereto by their refpective holders, and fhall, after the faid day,
ceafe to be exercifed elfewhere; and that the neceffary expence of fuch removal fhall be defrayed out of the duties on impofts and tonnage, of which a
fufficient fum is hereby appropriated.

, FREDERICK AUGUSTUS MUHLENBERG,
Speaker of the Houfe of Reprefentatives.
JOHN ADAMS, *Vice-Prefident of the United States,
and Prefident of the Senate.*

APPROVED, July the fixteenth, 1790.
GEORGE WASHINGTON, *Prefident of the United States.*

A 1790 act for establishing the temporary and permanent seat of the government
of the United States. *Library of Congress, Rare Book and Special Collections Division,
Printed Ephemera Collection.*

the opportunity offered them of deliberately deciding on the spot where the Capital City should be fixed."[10]

Unfortunately for the duo, the map would never be completed, at least not at the hands of L'Enfant. Washington felt pressured to have a blueprint of the city in a timely manner, while the Frenchman was a perfectionist and took time revising and rearranging his work. The president feared Congress would keep the seat of government in Philadelphia and even warned L'Enfant of the possibility.[11] After multiple disputes with the president and a prolonged plan submission to a Philadelphia engraver, Washington replaced L'Enfant with Ellicott, instructing him to finish the job.[12] The terrain where U Street would later be built stretched within the northern boundary of L'Enfant's primary outline for the city.[13]

Until 1871, the District of Columbia was separated into multiple districts: Georgetown, Washington City and Washington County.[14] Washington County was made up of Maryland lands, Washington City would later become the federal government area and Georgetown—same as today— was located near the Potomac River.[15] The city of Alexandria was also part of the District until the land was retroceded in 1846 to protect it from Washington's slavery mandates.[16] Lawmakers in the southern parts of the District were afraid that the antislavery sentiments rising in the heart of Washington would soon affect the Alexandria slave market, which was a major industry in the 1840s.[17]

These same fears pushed freedpeople into opposition of retrocession. Despite not having a vote in the matter, some freed Blacks spoke out against the retrocession. Moses Hepburn, a well-known Black businessman, wrote to New York abolitionist Gerrit Smith in agony, fearing fellow freed Blacks would be mistreated if the retrocession bill were to pass:

> *We have been permitted heretofore to meet together in gods sanctuary which we have erected for the purpose of religious worship. But wheather we shall have this priveledge when the Virginia laws are extended over us we know not, we expect that our schools will all be broken up* [and] *our priv-elidges which we have enjoyed for so maney years will all be taken away.*

Hepburn's predictions were accurate. For whites in Alexandria, the retrocession was beneficial, bringing about new railroads, banks, manufacturing and a powerful slave trade. Meanwhile, African American schools were closing because of Virginia's laws that prohibited the education of Blacks, thus the opportunities that were once available for free Alexandrians

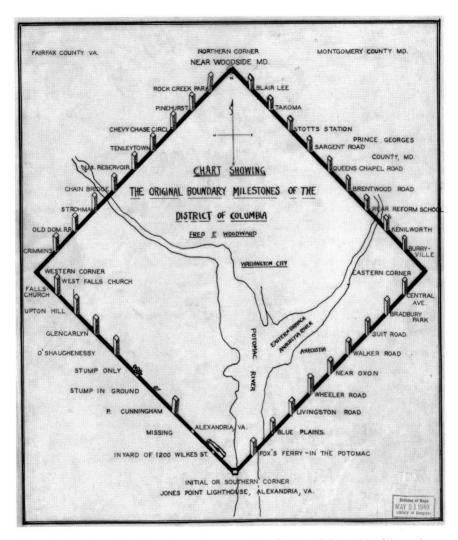

Chart showing the original boundary milestones of the District of Columbia. *Library of Congress, Geography and Map Division.*

diminished. The loss of rights for freed Blacks drove Alexandria's freedpeople to more liberal places like Washington and Georgetown.[18] Once Alexandria returned to Virginia, the population of free Blacks in Alexandria dropped 28 percent from 1840 to 1850.[19]

Virginia had every reason to fear the coming change in climate. Slavery in Washington was no secret, and by the early 1800s, some whites residing in Washington and some passing through were sickened by the sights of

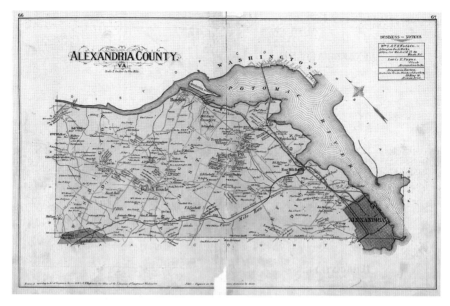

Atlas of fifteen miles around Washington, including the counties of Fairfax and Alexandria, Virginia. *Library of Congress, Geography and Map Division.*

slaves, handcuffed and shackled, treading throughout the capital. English traveler E.S. Abdy described his first encounter with a Washington slave pen as wretched in his 1835 journal. He wrote:

> *One day I went to see the "slaves' pen"—a wretched hovel, "right against" the Capitol, from which it is distant about half a mile, with no house intervening. The outside alone is accessible to the eye of a visitor; what passes within being reserved for the exclusive observation of its owner, (a man of the name of Robey,) and his unfortunate victims. It is surrounded by a wooden paling fourteen or fifteen feet in height, with the posts outside to prevent escape and separated from the building by a space too narrow to admit of a free circulation of air. At a small window above, which was unglazed and exposed alike to the heat of summer and the cold of winter, so trying to the constitution, two or three sable faces appeared, looking out wistfully to while away the time and catch a refreshing breeze; the weather being extremely hot. In this wretched hovel, all colors, except white—the only guilty one—both sexes, and all ages, are confined, exposed indiscriminately to all the contamination which may be expected in such society and under such seclusion.*[20]

Slave markets like the one Abdy witnessed were common in the city because the District stood as a major trading post situated between Maryland and Virginia. Washington markets sent Blacks from Chesapeake to the South—as far as Kentucky.[21]

The holding pens or slave pens served as places to temporarily keep slaves until it was time for them to be auctioned off. Conditions of these places were harsh, as Abdy noted. Numerous accounts of slave jails, holding pens and Blacks chained together in the streets were recorded by whites stunned and disgusted with the irony of massive bondage in a "free" capital.[22] Famed novelist Charles Dickens wrote about his visit to the capital in his literature *American Notes*. His first time being served by slaves was when he stopped to have dinner in Baltimore on his way to Washington. He recalls the dining

A Slave-Coffle passing the Capitol.

A slave coffle passing through the capitol around 1815. *Library of Congress.*

experience as shameful and repulsive: "The sensation of exacting any service from human creatures who are bought and sold, and being, for the time, a party as it were to their condition, is not an enviable one." Dickens also recorded seeing female slaves working at the hotel where he lodged in Washington and slave drivers "sunning" themselves in front of storefronts in the street.[23]

Even lawmakers in the city who may not have been totally opposed to slavery were gripped when catching a glimpse of slavery up close. In 1816, Virginia congressman John Randolph wrote, "In no part of the earth, not even expecting the rivers on the Coast of Africa was there so great, so infamous a slave market, as in the metropolis, in the seat of government of this nation which prides itself on freedom."

Not all of the whites who complained about the horrid sights of slaves were antislavery, some just thought the public visibility of bondage gave the city a bad reputation. Nonetheless, the growing distaste for the selling of Black humans created an awareness that sparked a national abolition movement.[24]

The wave of abolitionism took off in 1828, when one thousand citizens petitioned Congress to outlaw slavery,[25] but the progression of challenging slavery in D.C. dates further back. In 1801, Congress appropriated formal jurisdiction over the District, and just four years later, a resolution abolishing slavery was voted on by the House of Representatives but failed. Then, in 1808 and 1809, Congress placed a constitutional ban on importing slaves into America, but what seemed to be a step in the right direction actually caused an increase in the domestic slave trade.

In the midst of the Industrial Revolution, and with an increased demand for cotton and textile manufacturing, the slave trade in Washington expanded as southern slave owners needed more laborers from the Chesapeake area, which was a short distance from the North-South border.[26]

However, as the population of the enslaved in Washington increased toward the end of the eighteenth century, so did the population of freedpeople. Manumission laws in the city allowed slaves to purchase their own freedom, and laborers like Aletha Tanner took advantage of the opportunity. Tanner paid $1,400 for her liberty after earning money at a small market garden she started with the help of Thomas Jefferson. She eventually bought the freedom of twenty-two relatives and acquaintances.[27] This process, along with the Underground Railroad, a secret escape network for slaves, gradually lowered the slave population in Washington.[28] Despite hardships, free Black Washingtonians strived to better their race. They found work as carters, seamstresses and cooks.

In 1807, three illiterate Blacks, two employed at the Navy Yard, built a schoolhouse for children of color in Northwest, D.C. Three more schools for Black youngsters were opened throughout the District, one in Georgetown by British native Mary Billings, one by an Englishman and the other by a Black woman on Capitol Hill.

Whites and blacks continued to work together in the fight for equality or, at least, liberty.[29] In 1814, Black Methodists in Georgetown built Mount Zion with the monetary assistance of a religious white man. Free and enslaved Blacks had been worshiping together at the Montgomery Street Church as early as 1772, now called Dumbarton United Methodist Church, located on Dumbarton Avenue between Thirty-First Street and Wisconsin Avenue, Northwest. At its origin, Montgomery Street Church was located on Twenty-Eighth Street between M Street and Olive Avenue, Northwest, and Blacks and whites congregated together until some Black parishioners grew tired of discriminatory treatment. On June 3, 1814, 125 Black church members, dissatisfied with segregation, discussed the formation of a separate church. Henry Foxhall, a layman of Montgomery Street Church and wealthy Georgetown factory owner, sold to the founders a thirty-five-by-fifty-foot lot on Mill Street, now Twenty-Seventh Street, near West Street, now P Street. By 1816, the new church was established as Mount Zion, known at the time as the Meeting House or the Ark.[30]

The formation of Black churches in D.C. would continue in 1820. African American congregants at Ebenezer Methodist Episcopal Church, exasperated with their slave-owning pastor and segregation in the sanctuary, separated themselves from the white church and established the Israel Bethel Church, which later acquired a building on South Capitol Street. Blacks pushed to create a self-reliant community, but strict ordinances known as Black Codes would threaten to suppress their advancements.[31]

By 1830, there were more free Blacks in Washington than enslaved, and by 1850, there was a total of 4,694 slaves compared to 8,461 freedpeople. Still under the laws of Black Codes, freedpeople could be subject to arrest and sold into slavery if they were unable to provide proof of freedom.[32] For instance, in 1835, fourteen-year-old Nancy Jones was stopped by a police officer while walking down a street in the capital. Jones was asked to show her "papers," but the young girl, who was free and had never been a slave, did not have paperwork verifying her freed status. The policeman arrested her as a runaway slave, per the law at the time, and she spent months in jail, until her father's white landlord from Baltimore traveled to D.C. to testify in court for her release.[33] The codes leading to Jones's

A broadside condemning the sale and keeping of slaves in the District of Columbia in 1836. *Library of Congress.*

unfortunate arrest had grown stricter after an 1821 revision instituted by Mayor Samuel Smallwood and the Board of Aldermen,[34] and by 1835, the codes implemented a curfew of 10:00 p.m. for Blacks, as well as a $500 "peace bond" certifying good behavior. Certain ordinances were passed down from Maryland and Virginia, for example, a Black person could not testify against a white person, hold office or vote.[35] These laws also placed constraints on public gatherings. Chapter 53 of the *Ordinances of the Corporation of Washington* detailed the 1820 law:

> *The Corporation of Washington shall have power and authority, to restrain and prohibit the nightly and other disorderly meetings of slaves, free negroes and mulattoes, and to punish such slaves by whipping, not exceeding 40 stripes, or by imprisonment, not exceeding six months for anyone offence, and to punish such free negroes and mulattoes by penalties, not exceeding twenty dollars, for any one offence.[36]*

FIGHTING BACK

Antislavery groups, societies and newspapers were popping up throughout the country in cities like New York, Baltimore and Boston so rapidly that by 1827 there were 130 local abolition societies.[37] New Jersey native Benjamin Lundy, one of the first to publish an antislavery newspaper, launched a Baltimore branch of his publication, the *Genius of Universal Emancipation*, in 1829 and brought William Lloyd Garrison aboard as co-editor. The paper's content pushed the issues of enslavement in America.[38] Garrison later founded his own prominent publication in New England, the *Liberator*, in 1831. Garrison's publication was a call for an immediate end to slavery,[39] while Lundy worked toward gradual abolition.[40]

Both men were associates of the American Colonization Society, a group centered on the emigration of freedpeople to the west coast of Africa. Garrison eventually rejected the views of that organization.[41] The idea of relocating free Blacks was a suggestion that stemmed from the powerhouse slaveholding state of Virginia after the state's assembly adopted a resolution granting the governor power to ask the president for a place to relocate Blacks outside of the United States. This resulted in the formation of the American Colonization Society in 1816.

Headed by white New Jersey minister Robert Finley, the group viewed colonization as beneficial for both races. As the goals of the society, Finley listed, "We would be cleared of them; we would send to Africa a population partially civilized and Christianized…[and] blacks would be put in a better condition." Despite controversy surrounding such expeditions, the group had some success. In 1821, emancipationists and slaveholders resettled a number of Blacks to Liberia. And there were some Washington leaders, Black and white, in support of colonization, including two former presidents, James Monroe and James Madison, along with Supreme Court justice John Marshall and African American figures such as abolitionist and sea captain Paul Cuffee and journalist John B. Russwurm. Activist Mary Ann Shadd Cary,[42] who became the first Black woman to publish and edit a newspaper in North America, agreed with colonization for a time.[43]

Lundy used his paper to promote emigration, although he disagreed with sending Blacks to Africa. Lundy frequently searched for land in North America to find nearer options for resettlement, his preferences for locations being Haiti, Canada and the Mexican province of Texas.[44] By 1827, articles in opposition of colonization had begun to surface in the *Freedom's Journal*.

That same year, slavery was abolished in New York. The first Black-owned paper in the United States rolled out its first four-page, four-column issue in New York City on March 16. The editors, Samuel Cornish and Russwurm, immediately took a stance against the mainstream press and the misconceptions surrounding Black lives with their first issue:[45]

> *We wish to plead our own cause. Too long have others spoken for us. Too long has the publick been deceived by misrepresentations, in things which concern us early. It shall ever be our duty to vindicate our brethren, when oppressed, and to lay the case before the publick. We shall also urge upon our brethren (who are qualified by the laws of the diferent states) the expediency of using their elective franchise, and of making an independent use of the same. Useful knowledge of every kind, and every thing that relates to Africa, shall find a ready admission into our columns; and as the vast continent becomes daily more known, we trust that many things wil came to light, proving that the natives of it are neither so ignorant nor stupid as they have generally been supposed to be.[46]*

The journal worked to create a new culture for Black people outside of what white people had fabricated. Circulating in eleven states, the District of Columbia, Haiti, Europe and Canada, the articles advocated for voting rights, called for an end to lynchings, disseminated informative and educational news, profiled Black trailblazers and even published birth, death and wedding announcements.[47]

The momentum that abolitionists and rebelists were creating in Washington could not be ignored. There were so many uprisings and vocal

Benjamin Lundy to Andrew Jackson, September 4, 1823. *Library of Congress, Manuscript Division, Andrew Jackson Papers.*

Portrait of William Lloyd Garrison between 1870 and 1879. *Library of Congress.*

oppositions to slavery that, on May 26, 1836, with a vote of sixty-eight to seventeen, Congress passed a gag rule that shelved all petitions relating to slavery.[48] After Nat Turner's slave revolt of 1831 in Southampton County, Virginia, and the Pearl incident in 1848, where seventy-seven slaves sailed up the Potomac to the Chesapeake Bay in an attempt to run away, the nation's government scrambled to find a resolution to the openly controversial practice of enslavement.

As a member of the House of Representatives representing Illinois, Abraham Lincoln introduced legislation in 1849 to compensate slave owners in exchange for banishing the buying and selling of slaves in the District—not slavery as a whole. The bill did not pass, and Lincoln decided it was "useless to prosecute the business at the time."[49] One year later, the Compromise of 1850 was admitted after California petitioned Congress for permission to enter the Union as a free state outlawing slavery from its territory. Accepting a new free state interfered with the political balance between North and South that was previously negotiated in the Missouri Compromise of 1820 in which an imaginary line drawn west of Mississippi split the country in two, leaving northern states as free and southern states as slaveholders.[50]

To prevent a confrontation between the North and South over the spread of slavery, the compromise included five bills, one of which included an

Abraham Lincoln's bill to abolish slavery in the District of Columbia, published January 1849. *Library of Congress, Manuscript Division, Abraham Lincoln Papers.*

amendment to the Fugitive Slave Act and the prohibition of slave trading in Washington. At the time, the District was the biggest slave market in North America. Republican Senator Henry Clay from Kentucky took the lead on the proposal or package, known as an omnibus bill, and by September 1850, the compromise passed as law.[51] The Fugitive Slave Act made it illegal for Blacks and whites to assist, house, feed or clothe runaway slaves and required citizens to turn them in.[52] It also denied slaves the right to a jury trial. The law was viewed as biased in favor of southern states, but in some northern states, the law was practically unenforceable. This resulted in the Underground Railroad, a secretive network aiding runaway slaves, peaking during this time,[53] with D.C. being a haven for slaves fleeing from the border slave states Maryland and Virginia.[54] By 1860, approximately only 330 slaves had been returned to their masters, despite the Fugitive Slave Act.[55] In that same year, the majority of Washington's Blacks were out of bondage: "there were 75,080 whites living in the District along with approximately 14,000 blacks, 11,131 of whom were already free."[56] And the start of the Civil War in 1861 motivated more slaves to escape the South in hopes of finding emancipation on northern soil.

Above: A map detailing the 1850 Compromise. *Library of Congress, Geography and Map Division.*

Opposite: Fugitive Slave Act of 1850. *Library of Congress.*

462   THIRTY–FIRST CONGRESS. Sess. I. Ch. 60. 1850.

Sept. 18, 1850.

1793, ch. 7.

CHAP. LX. — *An Act to amend, and supplementary to, the Act entitled " An Act respecting Fugitives from Justice, and Persons escaping from the Service of their Masters," approved February twelfth, one thousand seven hundred and ninety-three.*

Commissioners to execute the powers and duties of this act.

1789, ch. 20.

Be it enacted by the Senate and House of Representatives of the United States of America in congress assembled, That the persons who have been, or may hereafter be, appointed commissioners, in virtue of any act of Congress, by the Circuit Courts of the United States, and who, in consequence of such appointment, are authorized to exercise the powers that any justice of the peace, or other magistrate of any of the United States, may exercise in respect to offenders for any crime or offence against the United States, by arresting, imprisoning, or bailing the same under and by virtue of the thirty-third section of the act of the twenty-fourth of September seventeen hundred and eighty-nine, entitled " An Act to establish the judicial courts of the United States," shall be, and are hereby, authorized and required to exercise and discharge all the powers and duties conferred by this act.

To be appointed by the Superior Court of each Territory.

Powers and duties.

SEC. 2. *And be it further enacted,* That the Superior Court of each organized Territory of the United States shall have the same power to appoint commissioners to take acknowledgements of bail and affidavits, and to take depositions of witnesses in civil causes, which is now possessed by the Circuit Court of the United States ; and all commissioners who shall hereafter be appointed for such purposes by the Superior Court of any organized Territory of the United States, shall possess all the powers, and exercise all the duties, conferred by law upon the commissioners appointed by the Circuit Courts of the United States for similar purposes, and shall moreover exercise and discharge all the powers and duties conferred by this act.

Courts authorized to enlarge the number of commissioners.

SEC. 3. *And be it further enacted,* That the Circuit Courts of the United States, and the Superior Courts of each organized Territory of the United States, shall from time to time enlarge the number of commissioners, with a view to afford reasonable facilities to reclaim fugitives from labor, and to the prompt discharge of the duties imposed by this act.

Jurisdiction of commissioners concurrent with that of judges, and shall grant certificates to take fugitives from service.

SEC. 4. *And be it further enacted,* That the commissioners above named shall have concurrent jurisdiction with the judges of the Circuit and District Courts of the United States, in their respective circuits and districts within the several States, and the judges of the Superior Courts of the Territories, severally and collectively, in term-time and vacation ; and shall grant certificates to such claimants, upon satisfactory proof being made, with authority to take and remove such fugitives from service or labor, under the restrictions herein contained, to the State or Territory from which such persons may have escaped or fled.

Duty of marshals and deputies.

Penalty for refusing to execute the same.

Liable for value of a fugitive escaping after his arrest.

SEC. 5. *And be it further enacted,* That it shall be the duty of all marshals and deputy marshals to obey and execute all warrants and precepts issued under the provisions of this act, when to them directed ; and should any marshal or deputy marshal refuse to receive such warrant, or other process, when tendered, or to use all proper means diligently to execute the same, he shall, on conviction thereof, be fined in the sum of one thousand dollars, to the use of such claimant, on the motion of such claimant, by the Circuit or District Court for the district of such marshal ; and after arrest of such fugitive, by such marshal or his deputy, or whilst at any time in his custody under the provisions of this act, should such fugitive escape, whether with or without the assent of such marshal or his deputy, such marshal shall be liable, on his official bond, to be prosecuted for the benefit of such claimant, for the full value of the service or labor of said fugitive in the State,

FIRST IN FREEDOM

In the month of May alone, just one month after the April 12, 1861 Confederate attack on Fort Sumter, seventy-three fugitives slaves were captured in the nation's capital and re-enslaved after seeking asylum in D.C.[57] Lincoln had been inaugurated as the sixteenth president of the United States five weeks before the attack. On April 15, 1861, he called for seventy-five thousand volunteers to join the Union in the fight against the South. African Americans correlated winning the war with achieving liberation, so they began organizing themselves into units, but the government initially refused to accept help from Black soldiers.[58]

Not only was the debate of slavery ongoing, but now Lincoln also needed more manpower to help defend the capital, so he turned toward freedpeople for aid. "The bare sight of fifty thousand armed and drilled Black men in uniform on the banks of the Mississippi would end the rebellion at once. And who doubts we can present that sight, if we but take hold in earnest," Lincoln once wrote to Andrew Johnson. Congress granted Lincoln's wishes in the spring of 1862, when the Senate and House of Representatives voted

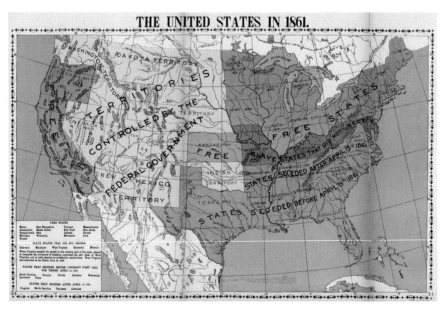

A historical map of the United States in 1861. *Library of Congress, Geography and Map Division.*

Print showing Abraham Lincoln in 1865. *Library of Congress.*

in favor of the bill titled Act for the Release of Certain Persons Held to Service or Labor in the District of Columbia by Reason of African Descent. The bill was signed into law by Lincoln on April 16, and the chains of all in bondage in the capital were loosed. Slaves in D.C. were emancipated by law, and slave owners were granted up to $300 in compensation per freed slave based on the $900,000 Congress allocated to reimburse the loss of

Forty African American soldiers sitting and standing on a slight hill near the Aiken house in Virginia in 1864. *Library of Congress.*

their property, along with a $600,000 national colonization fund to aid in the resettlement of freedpeople.

Black troops began to form regiments with help from recruiters like Frederick Douglass and Martin Delany.[59] On New Year's Day in 1863, Lincoln signed the Emancipation Proclamation freeing all slaves held in rebel states. This exempted the border states and parts of the Southern secessionist states that were already under Northern control.[60] However, the proclamation announced the enlistment of Black soldiers into the Union military. In May 1863, the Bureau of Colored Troops was formed after the president placed J.D. Turner and Reverend William G. Raymond in charge of the new regiment.[61]

The Civil War waged on until 1865, and by the end of it, nearly 200,000 blacks had served in the Union army and navy.[62] Douglass recorded that

City Point, Virginia African American army cook at work. *Library of Congress.*

the emancipation was the doom to slavery: "[N]ot only a staggering blow to slavery throughout the country, but a killing blow to the rebellion—and the beginning of the end for both."[63]

The Civil War tore the country in two, but in the midst of the division, the Black population in D.C. was on the rise as refugee slaves fled to contraband communities in the city. Out of these camps, social justice organizations, religious groups, schools and even medical centers manifested, paving the way for the framing of U Street's thriving Black culture. The establishment of the famed Howard University was soon to come.[64]

2

THE BLACK MECCA

Refugees, runaways, fugitives and clandestines[65] had a new name by the summer of 1861: Contraband. That's what the flood of Blacks fleeing slave owners and crossing Union lines were labeled during the Civil War. A new title for Black bodies—still property nonetheless—the question became whose property they were. Union general Benjamin F. Butler sought to answer this question after three slaves were presented to him following the seizure of Virginia's Fort Monroe, and as the commander, he refused to return the fugitives to the Confederates.[66] Southern states were using slave labor to support the Confederate army, and Butler reasoned that returning the runaways would be aiding the enemy. The Union general decided these slaves would be "contraband of war," and since they were loyal to the Union, they should be cared for by the United States government. "I should take the same care of these men, women and children—houseless, homeless and unprovided for—as I would for the same number of men, women, and children, who, for their attachment to the Union, have been driven or allowed to flee from the Confederate States," he explained to Major General Oliver Otis Howard after the war.[67]

Until Butler's declaration, slaves infiltrating Union lands looking for protection and shelter were to be sent back to their respective enslavers, regardless of which side they were supporting. With a major labor shortage and increased need for help in the war effort, army camps began using fugitive slave labor against the army headquarters' orders. The runaways were used for construction, cooking and, in some cases, as Confederate spies. This lasted until the Emancipation Proclamation.[68] The confiscation of slaves had been a controversial topic as Union politicians worked to find a solution and a justifiable way to capture Southern slaves without offending slaveholding border states who were in allegiance with the Union, like Maryland. So, on August 6, 1861, Congress passed the Confiscation Act authorizing the seizure and irreversible manumission of any slaves belonging to enemy masters. Those escapees owned by masters who were loyal to America would be returned to their owners under the Fugitive Slave Act of 1850. Contraband slaves were legally considered property of the U.S. government.[69]

Oliver Otis Howard, 1830–1909. *Library of Congress.*

Once Congress unchained the slaves in D.C. in April 1862, slaves from southern Maryland and Northern Virginia migrated to the District for work and shelter, especially once the military campaign began. In August 1862, as many as four hundred slaves arrived in the capital over a span of two days after the second Battle of Bull Run in Manassas, Virginia, to get away from the violence.[70] After June 1861, because of the influx of Black migrants to the area, the Washington Military District established a Contraband Department located at Twelfth and O Streets, Northwest.[71] The new department put freedmen to work on army forts, drawing the workers' families and loved ones to settle nearby.[72] More and more contraband camps surfaced throughout the city as the increase in refugees continued. Runaways made new homes in Union army encampments, warehouses and hospitals, settling in forts that had been built just after the war.[73] These havens became communities for Blacks. Although poverty stricken and disease infested, the camps gave newly freed Black people the opportunity to finally make a living of their own that would help them flourish in the twentieth century.[74] Scholar Joseph Reidy noted, "In the crucible of war, blacks in the capital area began the transition from dependence to independence, from slavery to freedom."[75]

Federal funding and aid from private organizations, such as the National Freedmen's Relief Association and Contraband Relief Association,[76] supported African Americans in exchange for labor. The able-bodied worked as government laborers, males as military laborers and servicemen

Contrabands migrating to camp in consequence of the proclamation on January 31, 1863. *Library of Congress.*

and those residents unable to perform strenuous tasks found work doing less cumbersome tasks like scrapping garbage from the streets,[77] gardening, making fires and cleaning.[78] Black soldiers earned a government fixed rate of ten dollars per month, but Black government employees were earning equal pay to whites, receiving as much as thirty dollars per month in addition to a daily ration, until a five dollar per month contraband tax on Black employees was instituted in September 1862 to curb camp operating expenses.[79]

One visitor, amazed with the professions available for freedpeople, in a collection of letters journaling his trip to Washington from New York, detailed, "Washington seems to be a kind of a Mecca for sable gentlemen." William J. Wilson, a contributor to *Frederick Douglass' Paper*, the *Weekly Anglo-African* and the *Anglo-African Magazine*, wrote in his September 5, 1863 letter:

> *It is to me no marvel now that colored men of the South have no disposition to remain North, and are ready to return as soon as the foul institution of slavery is swept away....Here in the South, it is blacks, blacks, blacks everywhere. Blacks on the government wagons—blacks on the drays—blacks on the hacks—blacks on the dirt-carts—blacks in the hotels, barbers shops, in all the houses, on all the streets. In the North we placed a high*

estimate upon the few crumbs thrown to us (for the service we rendered the Republican party to elect honest Abraham Lincoln), in the way of appointing a few colored men to places in the Custom House; but what think you of finding responsible colored men, by scores, employed here, in the Capitol, in the Treasury, in the State Department; in fine, in all the Departments of government; an acknowledgment of capacity, but more, an evidence of political recognition. With us in the North the employment of colored persons is the exception; here it is the rule.[80]

Wilson, who would later teach at a contraband school near the future U Street,[81] went on to describe the camps as boardinghouses for contraband or "a hotel for colored ladies and gentlemen." Although the refugee camps housed these "bronzed laborers," the conditions of living were far from the accommodations of a hotel.[82]

Initially built to lodge temporary inhabitants, problems arose when the shelters grew overcrowded with long-term residents. Sickness and disease plagued the residences. "I found men, women and children all huddled together, without any distinction or regard to age or sex....Many were sick with measles, diphtheria, scarlet and typhoid fever," Harriet Jacobs, former slave and abolitionist, said in her recollection of her visit to the District in the summer of 1862.[83] At one point, military officials, swamped by overpopulation, stuffed Blacks into the Old Capitol Prison, where they bunked with Confederate prisoners. The U.S. Supreme Court building is there now.[84]

In 1862, in an effort to combat overcrowding and a smallpox outbreak, boardinghouses along Duff Green's Row on East Capitol Street, where the Folger Shakespeare Library now stands,[85] were acquired by D.C. military governor James S. Wadsworth, but those filled up rapidly too.[86] The humanitarian crisis couldn't be contained, and Northern missionaries gravitated to Washington to help structure the emerging Black neighborhoods.

Just after the D.C. Emancipation Act, federal employees launched a local chapter of the National Freedmen's Association in a push to acclimate ex-slaves to society. The group's stated mission was "to teach [former slaves] Christianity and civilization; to imbue them with notions of order, industry, economy, and self reliance; [and] to elevate them in the scale of humanity, by inspiring them with self respect." Private missionary groups like the National Freedmen's Relief Association and American Missionary Association supported the contraband camps with fundraisers and staffers to supplement the minimal support that migrants received from the government.[87]

The center of the relief effort in Washington[88] was located at what is now a part of the U Street corridor. Positioned at what would become the intersection of Vermont Avenue at Twelfth Street, Northwest, Camp Barker,[89] sheltered some six hundred contrabands by the fall of 1862. Danforth Nichols, a Methodist minister from Boston, took the job of superintendent of contraband camps in June 1862, and one of his first duties was to construct Camp Barker. Before the war, the lot functioned as a cemetery and a brickyard, and with Nichols's supervision, the space became what he called the Washington Contraband Depot. Unfortunately, the new encampment didn't solve the plight of overpopulation as the flow of newcomers entering Washington continued. Barker residents remained in poor conditions cramped in ten-by-twelve-foot cabins lacking proper sanitation, restrooms and water.[90] Contraband camps were breeding grounds for diseases. According to D.C. history teacher Dr. Sharita Thompson, the improper conditions of the camps caused diseases to "spread like wildfire." Thompson said government officials tried to control infestation on the campgrounds by visiting sites and instituting cleanings that included things like washing down the walls and discarding excess newspaper.[91] In the summer of 1863, amid a smallpox epidemic, the camp averaged twenty-five deaths per week.[92]

The old Capitol prison, Washington, D.C. *Library of Congress.*

Portrait of General Robert E. Lee, February 18, 1865. *Library of Congress.*

By the end of 1863, campsites were banked on both sides of the Potomac River. There was the abandoned estate of Confederate general Robert E. Lee in Arlington, Virginia, known as Freedman's Village,[93] a camp next to the Navy Yard on the Southeast Anacostia River waterfront, another on Analostan Island in the Potomac River opposite Georgetown and Campbell Barracks near the future U Street on Seventh Street and Florida Avenue, Northwest.[94]

Barker eventually disbanded after Nichols partnered with military officials to transfer inhabitants to the new community in Arlington, which included fifty-two family homes, a pond, a hospital, a school, a chapel and a Home for Aged and Infirm Freedmen. Freedman's Village seemed to be a resolution to the overcrowding in the District, but 80 percent of Barker residents refused to leave their homes, as "they would rather starve in Washington than go to Arlington to be under Nichols," they confessed to a missionary. Overtime, Nichols had developed a paternalistic mentality toward Blacks, as did other white abolitionists in the relief effort.

Before emancipation, Black Washingtonians shared middle-class values with white counterparts as they worked together to fight for freedom, but the war brought a fresh class of African Americans into the city. The majority of fugitives were traveling directly from plantation life and coming to D.C. unemployed and uneducated, so white Northerners began to view new Black Washingtonians with sympathy, yet inferiority. Nichols, too, participated in

Freedman's Village, Arlington, Virginia, photographed between 1862 and 1865. *Library of Congress.*

the condescension, explaining, "To reason with them is out of the question. You must tell them what to do." Black critics viewed Nichols as a "tyrant" and "overseer," and once Camp Barker came to a close, more than five hundred of its inhabitants stayed in the area anyway.[95] After the war, these Barker homesteaders, already familiar with what is now U Street, settled where life was common and swelled into U Street and its surroundings, filling up alleyways and street residences.[96] Despite the controversy regarding the crippling of Black independence, over the course of the Civil War, as many as ten thousand escaped and liberated slaves obtained asylum in contraband camps, and the funding and missionary support that stemmed from these camps would also offer private education to Black refugees.[97]

FROM LABOR TO LEARNING

By 1864, more than two dozen day schools and eighteen night schools occupied Washington, totaling a Black student population of more than 4,600 students. One of these schools, formed and supported by aid societies and local churches, was the Camp Barker school. William Wilson, the only African American teacher employed in an American Missionary Association school in the area, taught at the Camp Barker school. After his employment, Wilson sought to hire only Black teachers. Wilson, alongside his wife, Mary, managed an average of about 250 students. The Wilsons worked to produce self-reliant Black citizens who could not only relish in being free but could also find strength and self-assurance in being autonomous. Wilson once told his bosses, "Colored people must be taught to do our own work, being assisted only by the dominant class….As long as the dominant class are to fill among us the first places, even when it can be avoided and we to be regarded as minors and recipients of favors we shall be but the same helpless and dependent people, slaves."[98]

In March 1864, the city's first Black public school opened. The following year, Congress established the Bureau of Refugees, Freedmen, and Abandoned Lands, better known as the Freedmen's Bureau. At a time when freedpersons were adjusting to the new life outside of bondage, the federal agency, placed in the War Department, sought to help Black people adapt to living apart from the plantation and oppressive masters. The first of its kind, the bureau dispensed aid directly to individuals under the responsibility to care for "all subjects relating to refugees and freedmen from rebel states," according to the mission. This collective focused on providing housing, education, employment and family reunification. White Connecticut abolitionist and women's rights advocate Josephine Griffing of the Freedmen's Bureau[99] reported that between 1865 and 1867, she helped find employment and housing in the North for about seven thousand Black Washingtonians.[100]

Still, the large influx of poor Blacks migrating to D.C. outweighed the support the government and private associations were able to provide, especially postwar, when being a soldier was no longer an available occupation.[101] And without being taught the principles of civilization, such as proper hygiene, literacy and thrift, even those with occupations were eventually subject to living in shambles, and freedmen without jobs were unable to pay rent at the government-owned low-rent tenements.

The city was in disarray.[102] The only permanent solution to successfully transition Blacks to independence was education. To add to the chaos, in the background of pushing for Black education, Radical Republicans were fighting for Black male enfranchisement. Against opposition from white critics like D.C. mayor Richard Wallach, a Democrat dismayed by Black progression, not only would suffrage be granted, but a university for all races was also born.

Postwar, Congress had overpowered the slaveholders and was now ruled by the Republican Party, who were eager to expand federal power after a bitter four years of war and the assassination of Lincoln, the party's first president. Looking to spread fairness throughout the city while simultaneously upsetting white Washingtonians, who radicals viewed as "rebels at heart," egalitarian policies were set in place to implement Black rights.[103] Out of these initiatives, Major General Oliver Otis Howard was appointed commissioner of the Freedmen's Bureau. Despite the rigid Washington social and political climate, the commissioner worked tirelessly to open medical facilities, housing developments and U Street's epicenter, Howard University.

"Naturally, as the great war drew to a close, I had been pondering the subject of my future work. Should I remain in the army or not? What as a young man of thirty-four had I better do? The opportunity afforded by this offer appeared to me at once to answer my anxious inquiries. Indeed, it seemed providential," Howard later noted while reflecting on accepting the leadership role. The devout general, with the help of the District's First Congregational Church, secured a congressional charter for Howard University in 1867, the same year Black males in D.C. received the right to vote.

THE FREEDMEN'S BUREAU.—Drawn by A. R. Waud.—[See Page 517.]

Man representing the Freedman's Bureau stands between armed groups of Euro-Americans and African Americans, created in 1868. *Library of Congress.*

For the high price of $1,000 an acre, Howard and his colleagues purchased the 150-acre farm of John A. Smith on a hill overlooking the city and built the first university south of the Mason-Dixon line committed to biracial education.[104] With initial investments by the Freedmen's Bureau, the campus featured a three-story, granite-foundation academic building with thirty-two classrooms, a dormitory for female boarding students named after antebellum educator Myrtilla Miner and the Freedmen's Hospital.[105] Private donations and student tuition fees of three dollars per term supplied funds for theology courses, a preparatory unit and, in 1868, medical and law schools.[106] At the start, the university named after Howard, who would serve as the college's third president,[107] had an all-white faculty. Its first graduates were four white women, who were daughters of faculty members,[108] and even the daughters of Nichols attended the school. Still, the teachings were dedicated to training Black students, who made up the majority of the population:[109] "The early posture as the nation's only true integrated university was reflected by Howard's original seal whose motto asserted, 'Equal Rights and Knowledge for All.'"[110] Under the general's governance, a curriculum of mandatory Greek and Latin was instilled,

Stereograph showing a crowd of African American students on the lawn of Howard University near Miner Hall. *Library of Congress.*

along with virtues of discipline and piety, setting a standard for the years to come.

In 1872, the Freedmen's Bureau shut down, but the university lived on.[111] Also known as the "Capstone of Negro Education," the coeducational school housed and groomed a number of Black intellectuals. Frederick Douglass was a member of the Howard Board of Trustees from 1871 until his death in 1895.[112] A surgeon and the highest-ranking Black officer in the Union army during the Civil War, Dr. Alexander T. Augusta directed Freedmen's Hospital,[113] which was located on Howard University's property at Fifth and W Streets, Northwest, from 1869 to 1975.[114] Augusta became the first African American to serve on the faculty on any medical school when he joined Howard's medical college.[115] Mathematician Kelly Miller helped organize a sociology department for the school in the 1890s.[116]

By the early 1900s, the college employed prominent faculty members, such as historian Carter G. Woodson, the originator of Black History Month, and famed lawyer Charles Hamilton Houston, also known as the "Man Who Killed Jim Crow."[117] Then, in 1926, the university's first Black president, Dr. Mordecai W. Johnson, was appointed. A major contribution of $231,627.39 was given to the institution that same year. Qualified Black educators were brought in to replace the white faculty, and the university received accreditation for all of its schools and colleges under the direction of Johnson.[118] In the early decades of Johnson's leadership, Howard University trained nearly half of the nation's Black

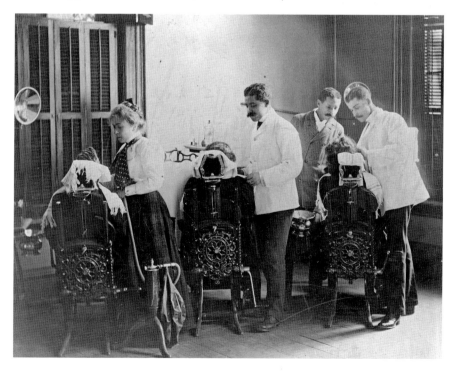

Howard University dentistry in 1900. *Library of Congress.*

physicians and dentists, and 96 percent of the nation's Black lawyers.[119] Economist Abram Lincoln Harris, Nobel Peace Prize laureate Ralph Bunche and sociologist E. Franklin Frazier all joined Howard's faculty under Johnson's headship.[120]

FROM A UNIVERSITY TO A NEIGHBORHOOD

From the early years of the Reconstruction era, Howard University attracted Black scholars, entrepreneurs and activists to D.C., fueling the trend of Black education and affluence to the point that the District had the largest Black population of any city in the country in the late 1800s. A Howard University Law School graduate, the second Black woman in the nation to earn a law degree,[121] educator and journalist Mary Ann Shadd Cary referred to the nation's capital as "the Mecca of the colored pilgrim seeking civil, religious, social and business enlightenment, and preferment or

Howard University classroom in early 1900s. *Library of Congress.*

Historic Victorian architecture at LeDroit Park, a neighborhood in Northwest, Washington, D.C. in 2010. *The George F. Landegger Collection of District of Columbia Photographs in Carol M. Highsmith's America, Library of Congress, Prints and Photographs Division.*

protection."[122] Howard, in particular, trained and hired some of the nation's most prominent African American thinkers, gaining the prestige of being America's top Black university by the 1880s.[123]

A Black community known as Howardtown surrounded the university and, by 1891, spilled over into the nearby white neighborhood of LeDroit Park, which had been built to be exclusive. The advertisements of the park promoted "no poor buildings" and "protection from all nuisances and undesirable features." For about the first twenty years after LeDroit's inception, it was completely white, but the presence of Howard attracted Blacks of different economic backgrounds and social classes to the U Street area, and by the early 1900s, African American homeowners flooded the vicinity, raising the bar from low-income Black workers to property owners. The U Street corridor, like many other D.C. Black neighborhoods, formed out of nearby contraband camps, destitute and restricted but with opportunities for Blacks on the rise. Leaders like activist Mary Church Terrell, champion of Black education Anna Julia Cooper and poet Paul Laurence Dunbar settled around U Street. However, the fight for equality was nowhere near over.[124] The innovators and revolutionaries who were either birthed of or lured to U Street would have to band together as lawmakers, radicals and elitists in the near future to defeat the coming opposition to Black advancement, Mr. Jim Crow.

3

THE GREAT BETRAYAL

The Fifteenth Amendment was a short-lived victory for Black males. "The right of citizens of the United States to vote shall not be denied or abridged by the United States or by any state on account of race, color, or previous condition of servitude" read the 1869 constitutional amendment. But by 1871, talks of a consolidated District of Columbia sought to snatch enfranchisement away from all Washingtonians, Black and white, one political diversion at a time.

Reconstruction began to spiral out of control as racism in the South heated up in response to the acceleration of Black achievement brought about by northern radicals. The Republican experiment of an interracial democracy brought about suffrage, state-funded public schools, more equitable taxation legislation and laws protecting Blacks from racial discrimination. Yet, as Blacks succeeded, white aggression stirred, and supremacist organizations like the Ku Klux Klan surfaced, using violence to intimidate Blacks. While lynchings in the South were instigated, District whites used a less barbaric approach in walking back the progression of Reconstruction, and it began with instituting a territorial government.[125]

A friend of President Ulysses S. Grant, Alexander Robey Shepherd, had a vision of economic development for D.C., and it consisted of shifting power into the hands of property owners only. The "Boss" was a Southwest D.C. native and a plumber, who in 1861, worked his way into politics. He was elected to city council with the support of fellow merchants to promote infrastructure improvements. In 1862, the ambitious man pushed for city

Ulysses S. Grant. *Library of Congress, Manuscript Division, Brady-Handy Collection.*

construction. "Make this metropolis worthy [of] the hallowed name it bears, and worthy to be the capital of the 'great Republic' of the world," he emphasized. By 1864, he was one of the District's wealthiest men, and since he was never a radical fan of African American rights when suffrage was granted to Black males in 1867, Shepherd made moves to preserve white supremacy and whites-only politics.[126] District residents were denied full voting representation in Congress, but Georgetown and Washington City elected mayors, council members and other local officials at the time. Women were still prohibited from voting altogether.

African Americans wasted no time voting once they were able. Men of color represented nearly half of the electorate in Washington City and a significant percentage of the Georgetown electorate by 1867.[127] The pride and progress of suffrage was summed up in Frederick Douglass and Reverend J. Sella Martin's, pastor of Fifteenth Street Colored Presbyterian Church near U Street, publication, the *New Era*: "Each feels that he is a part, and has an interest in, the welfare of the city, the District, and the nation."[128]

A large number of Black voters supported Shepherd and his ally D.C. mayor Matthew Emery, formally city alderman, as a promise of jobs and public works projects stood at the forefront of Shepherd's agenda. The high level of Black political engagement was shown in the attendance at weekly Republican ward meetings: "They looked to the Republican Party not only to pass legislation in their favor or to facilitate their acquisition of jobs but also as a medium of personal expression and civic education. They regarded political participation as a way of acclimatizing themselves to the procedures of democracy and, in a broader sense, to the culture of freedom."

The local discussions took place in Black schoolhouses and churches, including the Second Ward's Fifteenth Street Presbyterian Church. As church played a huge role in Black communities, it was also reflected in local government. Republican meetings would often open with prayer and the singing of hymns. In one instance, after a poorly attended Ward 2 (the U Street district is a part of this ward) Club meeting, it was suggested that notifications of upcoming gatherings be announced at church by "leading colored men" instead of in advertisements in newspapers because many parishioners were unable to read. African Americans felt a strong connection to the Republican Party, which had accelerated the race's progression during Reconstruction, something Shepherd would use to undermine the neo-politicians of color. Black Washingtonians believed the party expressed their needs and shared their values, and the Black community was in need of better infrastructure.[129]

D.C. neighborhoods were in desperate need of redevelopment after the war, and U Street was no exception. Whites were trying to distance themselves from their Black neighbors as city life became increasingly segregated. U Street was overcrowded due to the District's swelling population, and space and adequate housing was an issue. So, Blacks and whites of all occupations and classes settled along the corridor out of necessity, not racial harmony. U Street grew into an abnormal urban middle ground. This unintentional integration wasn't part of Shepherd's plan.[130] Shepherd believed that property owners, not the poor, should make decisions for the city. So, after months of counter-campaigning to weaken Radical Republicans' expansive democracy, the momentum of public elections came to a halt in 1871. With the backing of businessmen, bankers and real estate developers, the square-jawed man convinced Congress to dissolve the city's administrative boundaries completely. The District's three governments, Washington City, Georgetown and Washington County, merged into one administrative unit under the direction of presidential appointees.[131]

John Sella Martin on July 14, 1862. *Library of Congress, Manuscript Division, Abraham Lincoln Papers.*

Supporters of the territorial government argued that multiple jurisdictions delayed development, generated confusion and created overlapping, thus a single government led by commissioners would be more effective.[132] This removed self-governance in D.C., and an unelected board named the Board of Public Works was established. All local officials were appointed by the president, except for a small number who were elected to the lower house of the territorial legislature. As a result, municipal affairs became less accountable to Black and white residents. Before this, the city governments were allowed to pass municipal ordinances, raise taxes and set budgets, improve streets, construct sewers and make provisions for health and safety.[133] Now those responsibilities would be managed by the board, presidentially appointed Governor Henry Cooke, upper Legislative Council and the popularly elected lower House of Delegates, alongside a nonvoting representative in the U.S. House.

"The taxpayers of this city did not want elections of any kind, and had not wanted them for 20 years," Shepherd said in 1868. "We want an honest Board of Commissioners and no broken-down political demagogues." President Grant appointed Shepherd to the five-man board, and he quickly

The 1869 National Colored Convention in session at a Washington, D.C. meeting hall to discuss the condition of the Black race in the United States. *Library of Congress.*

took control, making it the most powerful entity of city government. Shepherd defended his new territorial government, claiming that 90 percent of taxpayers and property holders were in favor of the consolidation.[134] Yet virtually all Blacks were against the new structure. Black elites like Sella Martin, John F. Cook Jr. and George Vashon sharply opposed Shepherd's scheme to remove the Black vote.

At the National Convention of Colored Men in January 1869, Vashon, Howard University's first Black professor, negated the reform as "a base plot, designed to defraud the eight thousand freedmen therein of the elective franchise, and cheat them of their newborn freedom."[135] Vashon's suspicions were accurate. The coming storm would rid District residents of enfranchisement for almost one hundred years.

Although many African Americans distrusted Shepherd, he continued to gain their support through job opportunities and patronage. Black workers were hired for his public works projects, and several high-profile appointments

Workmen from a monument-cleaning company cleaning Alexander Robey Shepherd's statue at Fourteenth and E Streets, Northwest, in August 1942. *Library of Congress, Prints & Photographs Division, Farm Security Administration/Office of War Information Black-and-White Negatives.*

were filled by people of color. About one third of the territorial government appointees were Black: Frederick Douglass served on the Legislative Council, Virginia native John Mercer Langston, Howard University Law School's first dean and presidentially appointed U.S. minister to Haiti, was appointed to the Board of Health and John F. Cook was named the city's registrar.[136] Thus a majority of Black voters appreciated the economic development of the Shepherd era but remained skeptical of what these benefactions would cost in return.

GOODBYE DEMOCRACY

Cost is exactly what sank the territorial government. The Comprehensive Plan of Improvements had a proposed cost of $6.6 million ($864 million in current dollars) and required a $4 million loan that Washingtonians approved. And though extremely pricey, with the funding of taxpayers, the city construction began, and it was marvelous. Streets and streetcar lines were improved, sparking a rise in real estate. Laborers built more than 150 miles of city streets, 120 miles of sewers and 200 miles of sidewalks. Sixty thousand trees were planted, and about three thousand streetlamps were posted. Victorian mansions were erected to house the elite.[137] The *National Republican* published a series of Saturday articles praising the Northwest development in 1873. The closing editorial read, "This city of Washington, which was the disgrace of the country, has blossomed into a beauty and a loveliness so that it is to-day the most attractive city in the Union. Its capital has almost doubled, the value of its real estate has been increased nearly fifty per cent, and in substantial growth we have surpassed almost every community on the continent."[138]

The excessive spending displeased white conservatives, especially Democrats, as Republicans dominated the new House of Delegates. Furious and fed up with Shepherd's business tactics, critics accused the Boss of budgetless spending and bribing and manipulating Black voters. Although an 1872 congressional investigation presented Shepherd as nearly spotless, Shepherd continued to make more enemies, and the city's debt snowballed. "Controlling the poor colored man's vote, and making his labor depend on it, and using it against the property and people of this city, is what these men are themselves doing," one observer wrote in reference to Shepherd's leadership.

The financial difficulties were too much for the city to bear, and by early 1873, the spectacular public projects were standing but with no money left to pay for it. The government had to stop paying teachers, laborers and other city employees. Shepherd tried to resolve the matter with a levy of higher taxes and more bonds, but his federal support had already waned. The stock market crash of 1873, known as the Panic of 1873, turned Shepherd's arrears into a nightmare. Washington collapsed economically, and the Black community would have to pay the damages in more than one way.[139]

Freedman Savings Bank folded post-crash, after being established in 1865 to help freedpersons save money and obtain property. Black depositors and organizations lost their savings. Howard University dropped courses and cut faculty salaries in half to avoid closing after being overburdened with debt.[140] The chaos prompted another investigation, and this time there was evidence of overspending, peddling and corruption.[141]

Democracy in the District came to an end on June 20, 1874.[142] Congress terminated the territorial government, abolishing Washington's nonvoting congressional representative along with it. The investigative report blamed District voters, Blacks especially, for allowing the disastrous legislature in the first place, as well as the careless spending. The territorial government had been put in place by "ignorant Negro voters," the publication the *Nation* explained, and the city should be controlled by those who are more responsible going forward. Although only two House of Delegates members out of twenty-two were Black and none of Shepherd's close advisers were Black, conservative Democrats still used the collapse as a way to claim Blacks were unfit for self-government. Thus a presidentially appointed board of three commissioners was established to manage the city and would be in charge of paying the debts. One member was required to be a member of the U.S. Army Corps of Engineers, and the other two spots were split between Democrats and Republicans. Washington became a "government city without a city government," one white observer, Mary Logan, said.[143] In September, the new commissioners used their first day in office to enact a law establishing chain gang labor on municipal projects, a sample of the Black indignities to come.[144] African American progress would continue to be walked back by conservatives with the Compromise of 1877.

Reconstruction shattered three years after Congress passed the disenfranchisement bill, when the Compromise of 1877 removed federal troops from the South.[145] The 1873 national depression had swallowed the majority of the South in poverty, and Democrats took control of the House of Representatives for the first time since the Civil War. In 1875, President

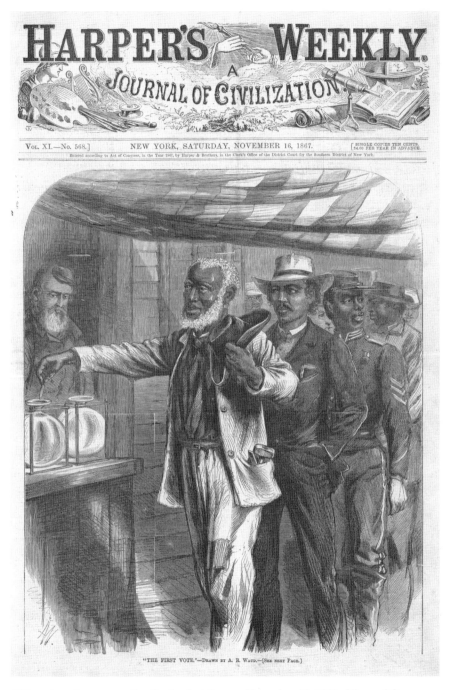

African American men voting for the first time on November 16, 1867. *Library of Congress.*

Grant refused to send federal troops to Mississippi when Democrats wanted to use violence to overtake the southern state. This marked the end of federal assistance in the South.

The Compromise of 1877 was established during the November 1876 presidential election when twenty disputed electoral votes were granted to Republican candidate Rutherford B. Hayes[146] in exchange for relinquishing the entire South to Democratic control.[147] Having a Republican president was more valuable than preserving Black freedom as this exchange jumpstarted a rollback of federal policies protecting equal rights for former slaves.[148] In a generation, voting restraints had passed in every southern state legislature.[149] Just a year after the compromise, the Organic Act of 1878 made the initially temporary commissioner structure of D.C. government permanent.[150] Suffrage, Frederick Douglass told the *Star*, was "the greatest protection of my race,"[151] and now that security had vanished. Washington wouldn't again revive the liberty of Reconstruction until the civil rights movement ninety-nine years later.

JUMP JIM CROW

The gradual yet consistent drawback of African American rights made way for the southern-based segregation system of Jim Crow.[152] About disenfranchisement, the *Nation* wrote, "Under this bill not a vestige is left of popular municipal government: aldermen, common councilmen, mayors, boards of works, school boards, police boards, primaries, conventions, all are swept away, and the entire government is handed over to three men, appointed by a foreign authority, responsible not to their fellow citizens, but to the President and Senate." The loss of elections wounded both Black and white voters, but for Washingtonians of color, the impact was most crippling. Black laborers were denied city contracts, and Black leaders had a tough time holding city officials accountable since higher-ups no longer needed to win over the votes of the people. The all-white commissioners, as all would be until 1961, dismissed the increasing rates of Black poverty, overlooked Black concerns and removed Blacks from city appointments. The struggle for Black people became so great during this time that 80 percent of U Street's Freedmen's Hospital patients were considered "too poor to pay for health care," while the Black infant mortality rate was 338.5 per 1,000 births.

As if the poverty and health conditions weren't devastating enough, blatant racial discrimination and racial hostility clouded the area too. Anti-Black police brutality increased, as only one Black officer was among the fifty appointments to the police force, and no Black men held firefighter positions in 1879.[153] Biracial meetings and political associations ended just as soon as they began, as social intercourse was no longer needed since the polls had permanently closed. All the while, Black migrants continued to enter Washington in record numbers as D.C. became increasingly segregated. Washington's overall population more than doubled from 1860 to 1880. The African American population skyrocketed from 14,328 to 59,596.[154] Relations between whites and Blacks were continuously tense, and eventually the division grew from among the two races to among those of the same color. Blacks bogged down with discrimination began to lose their stamina in standing up for one another.[155] Author Constance McLaughlin Green described the times as "vicious":

> *As time went on, white conviction that most blacks had failed to develop a sense of responsibility disillusioned formerly well-disposed whites who professed to think they had more than discharged their obligations to colored people. That disillusionment fed racial hostility as surely as racial discrimination undermined Negroes' determination to help themselves. The result was a vicious spiral. Whites concluded that most Negroes would never make good citizens, and Negroes, feeling themselves steadily shoved further into a corner by prejudice, ceased to stand up for one another and let the fight degenerate into that of each for himself.[156]*

Others would sum up the outcome of disenfranchisement in three words: "the great betrayal."[157] This was a major turning point for not just D.C. but also all Americans as the country entered a new era of racial hierarchy in the 1880s. Blacks had survived slavery, pushed past Black Codes, managed to gain employment and education and even served in Congress, but Mr. Crow would be around to stay for almost another century. Gleaned from a stereotypical character created by famed white minstrel singer Thomas "Daddy" Rice, "Jim Crow" was a term for racial belittling used by whites to disparage and demean African Americans. Starting as a performance of mockery and buffoonery in 1828, singing the tune "Jump Jim Crow," Rice danced and mimicked African American vernacular while wearing blackface. The song turned Rice into a successful entertainer, but for Blacks, there was nothing giddy about Jim Crow, as the term became shorthand to define customs, etiquette and laws purposed to segregate Blacks throughout the United States from the 1880s to the 1960s.[158] U Street was just one of many communities affected by the changes.

From the establishment of the Organic Act to the end of World War I in 1918, the area underwent multiple transformations as Jim Crow regulations, whether enforced by law or practice, strained District Blacks into segregated neighborhoods.[159] The ordinances drew an invisible color line in D.C. that created a vibrant Black middle class alongside alleyway neighborhoods for low-income Blacks out of economic necessity.[160] Whites sought residences farther north, distancing themselves from African American neighbors, while discriminatory practices such as inflated rent prices for Black buyers pushed people of color into self-same neighborhoods. "As the real estate boom in northwest Washington gained momentum, colored people moved farther from the center of the city. Whether sheer economics or, as rumor had it, combinations of real estate agents kept respectable Negroes from moving into desirable localities, the result was the same.…By 1900 the barrier of caste, seemingly collapsing in the later 1860s, had become stronger than ever," McLaughlin Green observed.[161]

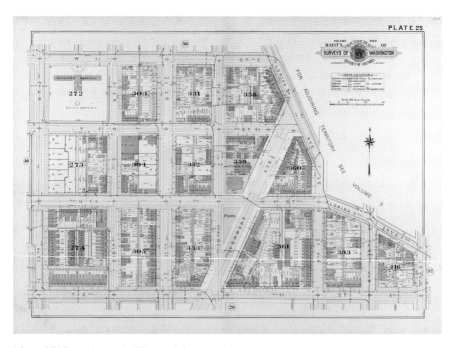

Map of U Street in 1903. *Library of Congress, Geography and Map Division.*

By 1900, the previously integrated U Street neighborhood of 1880 had become a "colored" neighborhood. After the Supreme Court ruled the Civil Rights Act of 1875 unconstitutional in 1883, segregation laws swept through the South. The outlaw of that bill, which had guaranteed equal access to public services and transportation, did not include Washington until a subsequent ruling in 1914, as D.C. is not a state.[162] Still, the minute the equal protection laws were rolled back in the South, Washington Blacks experienced the blowback. The system was supported by a belief that whites were superior to Blacks. The Jim Crow norms were pervasive, including:

- A Black male could not offer his hand (to shake hands) with a white male because it implied being socially equal. Obviously, a Black male could not offer his hand or any other part of his body to a white woman because he risked being accused of rape.
- Blacks and whites were not supposed to eat together. If they did eat together, whites were to be served first, and some sort of partition was to be placed between them.
- Under no circumstance was a Black male to offer to light the cigarette of a white female. That gesture implied intimacy.
- Blacks were not allowed to show public affection toward one another in public, especially kissing, because it offended whites.
- Jim Crow etiquette prescribed that Blacks were introduced to whites, never whites to Blacks. For example: "Mr. Peters [the white person], this is Charlie [the Black person], that I spoke to you about."
- Whites did not use courtesy titles of respect when referring to Blacks, for example Mr., Mrs., Miss, Sir or Ma'am. Instead, Blacks were called by their first names. Blacks had to use courtesy titles when referring to whites and were not allowed to call them by their first names.
- If a Black person rode in a car driven by a white person, the Black person sat in the back seat or the back of a truck.
- White motorists had the right-of-way at all intersections.

The Jim Crow statutes were even more excruciatingly enforced legally and were often defended with intimidation and violence. The most volatile repercussions occurred in southern and border states, where Black men and women were hanged, shot, castrated, dismembered and burned at the stake. Southern states alone account for nine-tenths of lynchings between 1889

A backyard in the slums of Washington, D.C., in July 1935. This backyard is typical of a group of houses very close to the House Office Building, which shows the only available water supply. *Library of Congress, Prints & Photographs Division, Farm Security Administration/Office of War Information Black-and-White Negatives.*

and 1940.[163] For Washington, the Jim Crow legislation was not adopted, but the rules, less harsh than southern states of course, still applied more so out of custom than actual mandate.

The 1896 *Plessy v. Ferguson* Supreme Court decision to uphold the 1890 Louisiana law of "providing for separate railway carriages for the white and colored races," set a new standard for constitutional separation. The court ruled that having "separate but equal" public facilities did not violate the Fourteenth Amendment because the amendment protects civil and political rights—not social rights. So, the 1896 verdict became the law of the land, and public places, including intrastate railroads, bathrooms, buses, schools, hotels, theaters and swimming pools were all lawfully segregated.[164] Washington, too, began to function as a racially segregated city after the mandate. Discriminatory practices like separate schools and residences and exclusions from shops and restaurants were increasingly sanctioned out of custom and physical force as white city commissioners turned a blind eye to questions on public access. The seclusion shoved Washingtonians of color into alley communities, where conditions were harsh, cramped and crime ridden.

ALLEY LIFE

Around the corner of Eleventh and R Streets, Northwest, the area once known as In the Woods had taken on the name of Hell's Bottom. Hell's Bottom, near today's Logan Circle, stood as a major vice and crime center. The neighborhood went from 54 percent white in 1880 to 85 percent Black in 1900 and was one of several District alley communities suffering from overcrowding.[165] Nearly a quarter of the city's African American population lived in alleys. By 1897, a police department special census found 18,978 alley residents in D.C., 93 percent of whom were Black. Similar to the earlier issues of contraband camp conditions, these alley dwellings formed out of eighteenth-century camps still had no indoor plumbing, little ventilation and little space. The geography of D.C. consisted of large blocks with narrow alleys. Along the street fronts stood row houses usually occupied by middle- and upper-class residents. In the alleyways, one- and two-room shanties were occupied by the working class. As migration into the city expanded, realtors began to place more alley residences in the backstreets. These "blind alley"

View of an alley dwelling in Washington, D.C., in September 1935. *Library of Congress, Prints & Photographs Division, Farm Security Administration/Office of War Information Black-and-White Negatives.*

The backyard of an alley dwelling home near the House Office Building in July 1935. The photo shows the privy on the right with the water supply between the privy and icebox. These tiny, unsanitary conditions were typical of Washington's overcrowded alleys. *Library of Congress, Prints & Photographs Division, Farm Security Administration/Office of War Information Black-and-White Negatives.*

homes were accessible only by way of another alley, creating neighborhoods completely hidden from street view.[166] U Street molded into a center of civilization in the early 1900s, although the conditions of the corridor would suggest otherwise.

By 1894, Congress had begun to place restrictions on alley construction because of the poor and unhealthy conditions. Organizations like the Board of Health and Washington Civic Center condemned the quality of life in alleyways. In 1934, Congress established the Alley Dwelling Authority "to provide for the discontinuance of the use as dwellings of the buildings situated in alleys in the District of Columbia."[167]

Despite the overall perception of alley residences, Black camaraderie formed among these hidden homes. "Alley life was hard, but the alleys also fostered a resilient sense of community. Like a modern suburban cul-de-sac, alleys offered a quiet haven far from the bustling street, a place where everyone knew everyone else and adults could pass time visiting on the stoop as the children played in the street," author Chris Myers Asch explained. The "alley people" depended on one another for childcare and other support; they were subdivided by segregation, but the isolation created an irony of unity.[168] The area of Hell's Bottom upgraded to Quality Row as Blacks worked to improve their environment. The racial barriers constructed by whites inspired Black Washingtonians to fend for themselves, and by the turn of the century, African American businesses and community groups began to form and flourish throughout the U Street corridor.[169]

4

STICK-TO-IT-TIVENESS

fter 1901, not a single Black man remained in the U.S. Congress as Jim Crow laws continued to pass throughout the nation. Color restrictions were set in Washington public establishments, with the exceptions of streetcars (Maryland segregated streetcars in 1903) and library reading rooms.[170] The intensity of segregation pressed D.C.'s African Americans into a single organized community. If Blacks were going to survive in this new era, they'd have to stick together, so that's what they did.

Since the founding of Washington, Black residents worked as store clerks, cab drivers, mechanics and craftsmen, but after the 1880s, Black commerce in D.C.—U Street in particular—increased tremendously. In 1886, there were only fifteen African American businesses in U Street's Shaw neighborhood, between Seventh and Fourteenth Streets, Northwest. Shaw was named after the area's junior high school in the mid-1960s, and its boundaries were redrawn to encompass 105 city blocks, including O Street Market and Mount Vernon Square, which extends closer to downtown D.C.[171] By 1920, the number of businesses rose to more than three hundred. The area was changing, and a new attitude toward Black business was forming—a new attitude of self-preservation. White racism made citywide resources unavailable for Blacks. The response was a build out of Black-made and Black-funded success. Black businessmen and women opened food establishments, retail stores, barbershops, banks, funeral homes and recreation centers; formed nonprofit groups; designed theaters and dining halls; constructed hotels and apartment complexes; sold automobiles; published magazines; and produced plays.[172] It was the beginning of not just an influx of Black business but also Black affluence that would go on to compete with other Black neighborhoods like New York's Harlem well into the Jazz Age.

Advocates for Black advancement encouraged racial solidarity in the face of white discrimination. In 1892, 1894 and 1895, the Union League of the District of Columbia published business directories urging Blacks to patronize businesses of color only.[173] After the Grand Opera House reinstated segregation in the theater and forced Black customers to the balcony in November 1899, Frederick Douglass's son Charles called for a boycott. The veteran and former president of the Bethel Literary and Historical Society incited African American patrons to "build your own theaters as you do your churches.…Are we forever to be dependent upon the whites for theaters, hotels, cafés, and stores of all descriptions?" he questioned.[174]

U Street's Black community answered with massive enterprises. There was former slave turned educator Anthony Bowen's Twelfth Street YMCA at 1816 Twelfth Street, Northwest, near the corner of Twelfth and S Streets, which opened in 1912. Bowen's branch had provided community services for people of color since its establishment in 1853 as the first Black branch of the national organization. There was the True Reformer Building built in 1903 at the corner of Twelfth and U Streets, which was designed by America's most prominent African American architect, John A. Lankford. The Laborer's Building and Loan Association at Twelfth, later Eleventh, and U Streets[175] stood a street over from the Whitelaw Hotel at Thirteenth and T Streets. What is now Ben's Chili Bowl used to be a movie theater called the Minnehaha at Twelfth and U, and the Lincoln or "first run" movie house opened next door in 1922, featuring live performances in the basement of the building called the Lincoln Colonnade. In 1912, the most popular Griffith Stadium ballpark, presently Howard University Hospital, was constructed.[176] There were places to live, board, dance, party, study, shop and play sports all within the U Street corridor. Writers Chris Myers Asch and George Derek Musgrove described the racial parallels of the early 1900s:

> *Where once they had sought entry into white clubs and organizations, often excluding the black poor, now black leaders created their own parallel groups. Where once they sought to win white approval by strenuously accentuating the differences between themselves and the black working class, they now created cross-class alliances to strengthen the entire community. Where once their wealth depended primarily on white benefactors, now their fortunes increasingly were linked to the black working class through business and community institutions.*[177]

White businessmen often refused to work in Black neighborhoods, leaving the market open for Black businesses to take advantage of, but opening a business required capital, something whites were reluctant to supply. White banks would accept deposits for Black customers, but few offered loans. Black borrowers typically paid 2 percent more than whites in interest for standard loans, 14 percent more for mortgage loans and at least 25 percent more for second mortgage loans. White property owners taxed Black businesses with higher rents, and white merchants jacked up the prices of wholesale goods when selling to Black clients.[178]

Financial institutions servicing Blacks were founded during these times of discriminatory customs and limitations, including the National Negro Business League; the Capital Savings Bank (where Mary Church Terrell's husband, Robert, was an officer); the True Reformers' Bank (established in Richmond); and the Industrial Building and Savings Association (one of which still stands today). The banks helped Black people get home loans, open savings accounts and deposit cash for Black businesses. Industrial Bank, in particular, still resides on U Street after several reorganizations and openings of other branches throughout the metropolitan area. The banks also hired Black tellers. Virginia Ali, the cofounder and owner of U Street's landmark Ben's Chili Bowl, got her start in D.C. at Industrial Bank. Ali had traveled from the South to D.C. to find work, like many southern women did during this time, and landed a job at a bank that was just a few doors down from her own future restaurant. Ali recalled meeting well-off African Americans while working as a clerk at Industrial Bank:

> *I remember a deposit from one of our architects once. I don't know who paid him this kind of cash money—must have been a number backer or something because we had number backers too—and this lady came in with $20,000 cash deposit. Back in those days, $20,000 would be like $115,000 in cash. And she was his secretary, and the way she walked in the bank, she had a grocery bag from the Safeway like she's got groceries and then reaches down in there and pulls out all that money. He was an architect. We had lots of architects; we had big-time real estate brokers; we had a very high-end middle-class community of people here [U Street].[179]*

FINALLY "LIVING OUT"

During the nineteenth century, women of color worked as "live-in servants," scrubbing floors, washing clothes, preparing meals and caring for children. Domestic work jobs were the only occupations for Black women at the time, and the hours were long and earned very little pay. The all-day and all-night stay-in jobs would pay about twenty-five cents per month. Girls in the South were trained as early as four years old for domestic work skills. Many of them migrated to D.C., where they used their childhood training to make a living in the city as adults.[180] Despite the literacy boost of the Reconstruction era, Black women remained limited to housework. At the turn of the twentieth century, roughly 90 percent of employed African American women worked as domestic servants. "A kitchen was where a colored woman got work....There's not a thing else for you to do. Just clean, cook, and hope for a change," D.C. migrant Geneva Wilson voiced after arriving in the District with a teacher's certificate from Tuskegee Institute, a Black school founded by Booker T. Washington in 1881.[181] In the 1920s, change finally came. A rise in apartment living and new technology for

A sewing class at Howard University in 1900. *Library of Congress, Prints & Photographs Division.*

maintaining the home with the use of electricity meant white employers no longer needed around-the-clock live-in staff. African American women transitioned from "living in" to "living out."

Women of color went from living with white employers to laboring as dayworkers, where they were able to get paid at the end of every day, have a schedule and work multiple jobs and homes. Prior to this, in most cases, wages were paid to a male family member or sent to kin in their hometowns. Daywork, although still very busy, granted Black women new freedoms. The ladies were even able to wear their own choice of clothing to the workplace, something that made domestic workers relatively equal in status to working-class Washingtonians. Earning more of their own money allowed some of the women to move out of their family homes and into boardinghouses or share rooms with friends. The newfound independence was exciting for former live-in servants, as they were now able to take days off, attend church, go to nightclubs, visit the zoo and spend nights at home with their children and, as one D.C. worker recalled with relief, finally sleep "in my own bed."

With a bit more free time, the hard workers were able to join in the social events happening around town at various churches. The increase in participation would lead to the emergence of Washington civic associations and clubs. Clubs and organizations grew as more dayworkers used their days off to attend meetings and socialize with government workers, teachers and laundresses. Laundresses were known to have more flexible schedules than live-in servants. Former live-in servant Isetta Peters described participation in her local church:

> When people got daywork, that's when my church started having clubs. Before then, most people didn't have no time. That church was closed up except on Thursday night. After people got more day-only work—that's when all these clubs, circles, and aid groups got going. Now church is open every night for them meetings![182]

U Street churches stood at the heart of spiritual, civic, social and political life for all ages. There were church-sponsored sports teams, theatrical plays, musical productions, picnics and parties. Even the first African American to perform with a major European opera company, D.C. native and Howard University graduate Madame Lillian Evanti,[183] performed concerts at local churches. Churches regularly hosted mass meetings for Black people to organize and discuss political and social issues. Later on, this would make an impact in the 1930s and 1940s, when U Street worship centers served as auditoriums for early civil rights activities.[184] The assemblies were usually in response to a specific incident, like a lynching in the South, or a racist comment made by a local official. Since Blacks could no longer vote, the meetings were ways to attract the media and voice their concerns. Outspoken Washingtonians expressed their concerns at churches, staged protests and signed petitions. One of the most prominent voices of the time was Mary Church Terrell, who frequently testified before congressional committees on behalf of people of color.

MRS. TERRELL

Terrell was born in 1863 in Memphis, Tennessee, to former slaves who eventually became successful business owners. The Terrells were among the wealthiest African Americans in the country. Terrell, rare for most women of her time, was highly educated, earning both a bachelor's degree and master's degree in classics from Oberlin College. After college, she spent a few years in Europe studying foreign languages and moved to D.C. in 1890 to teach at the Preparatory School for Colored Youth located in the U Street neighborhood.[185] The school mostly known as M Street High School, renamed in honor of poet Paul Laurence Dunbar in 1917, bred and hosted a number of Black educators, activists and elitists under the initial leadership of Superintendent George F. Cook. According to Constance McLaughlin Green, "Twenty of the thirty regular teachers had degrees from top-flight Northern colleges and universities and five others had graduated from Howard, a far larger proportion of highly trained talent than the white high schools could claim."[186]

One of the teachers was Harvard-educated Robert Terrell from Virginia. Robert and Mary met at M Street High School and married in 1891, becoming one of the city's most prestigious Black couples. The power couple lived in the esteemed Black neighborhood LeDroit Park near Howard University, a community that was also home to author and M Street mentor Anna Julia Cooper.[187] After marriage, Mary continued to work in education despite D.C. school regulations forbidding married women from teaching. With the encouragement of Frederick Douglass the tall, slim, fair-skinned woman continued her career and, in 1896, founded the National Association of Colored Women. She was also a founding member of the NAACP. She

Portrait of Mary Church Terrell between 1880 and 1900. *Library of Congress.*

was then appointed to the city's board of education, becoming the first Black woman in the nation to serve on a school board.

Having the advantage of living in D.C., where opportunities for Blacks were more available than in the South, Terrell became a renowned critic of white hostility. She was a member of Washington's African American upper class, writing for various publications and speaking out on women's suffrage and race relations. Her husband also added to their status of Black sophistication. During the time when the federal government was still a major employer of Black people, President Theodore Roosevelt appointed Robert as D.C.'s justice of the peace in 1901 and later promoted him to serve as the nation's first Black federal judge.

At the time, Blacks could even challenge white authorities in court and win, but with Jim Crow practices flooding the South and trickling to the North, the reality remained that Blacks were ultimately powerless in comparison to their white counterparts.[188] *Harper's Weekly* reporter Henry Loomis Nelson wrote in 1892, "But whether the black of Washington was free or slave, or the offspring of bondmen or freemen, he is kindly treated at the capital, treated as we treat irresponsible children."[189]

The autonomy for Blacks in D.C. was definitely not power. As poet and LeDroit Park resident Paul Laurence Dunbar explained in 1900, "Negro life in Washington is a promise rather than a fulfillment."

The federal government offered middle-class salaries for Black clerks and professionals, but life outside of the upper and middle classes was harsh. Manual federal government laborers earned little pay and few benefits. The municipal District government hired only 9 Black clerks out of the 450 city clerks, while there were only 9 Black firefighters out of the city's 398 firefighters. Mary Church Terrell, due to her social status, was sheltered from the effects of Jim Crow, but it didn't quell her resentment at the limitations for Black people just because of skin color. So, she, along with other Black activists, rich and poor, created their own schools, professional associations, literary societies and safe spaces to defy Jim Crow.[190]

NOT COLOR BUT CHARACTER

A younger generation of Black leaders were coming of age in the District, and their views differed from the influencers of color from the Civil War era. These new leaders included the editor of the *Washington Bee*, William

Calvin Chase, a Shaw resident with a home near Twelfth Street and Vermont Avenue; editor of the *People's Advocate*; John Wesley Cromwell, who lived in Shaw on Swann Street near Fourteenth Street;[191] and the first president of the Negro Academy, Reverend Alexander Crummell,[192] who had experienced the victories of emancipation. Mary Church Terrell and her peers had only known the bitter taste of segregation and disenfranchisement. Convinced that whites were unwilling to grant racial equality, the new generation of activists pushed for Black self-sufficiency. With a powerful sense of racial pride and youthful agility, they went on a mission to create and sustain their own organizations. Writer Kathryn S. Smith described the U Street neighborhood during this period as close knit: "Shaw was a dense weave of personal acquaintances and lifelong friendships based in strong families, churches, schools, fraternal and social clubs, black owned businesses, and other local institutions. These provided the support, training, and opportunities for important individual and group achievements."[193]

There were successful sporting clubs and recreational centers too. In 1905, named after the first African American female poet, Phyllis Wheatley, a YWCA (Young Women's Christian Association) branch was opened at Ninth Street and Rhode Island Avenue, Northwest. It offered community services to women of color, including a cafeteria, recreation center and banquet hall. The D.C. branch grew out of a Booklovers Club and has been referred to as the "heart of Shaw." Leading up to World War I, Anthony Bowen's YMCA basketball team dominated as the first African American basketball league in the country. In 1912, Clark Griffith built a stadium for his baseball team near Howard University. The ballpark attracted fans to U Street for half a century, playing home to such baseball teams as the white Senators and the Black LeDroit Tigers and talented Homestead Grays, as well as the Redskins football team, now known as the Washington football team.[194]

Standout leader of the "new business movement" and Howard University Law School student Andrew F. Hilyer began publishing the *Union Directory* in 1892 to help cultivate Black commerce. By 1901, Hilyer's directory catalogued more than 1,000 Black-owned businesses in D.C. In 1894, there had been only 120. Contributing organizer of the National Colored Press Association, which in 1894 became the National Afro-American Press Association.[195]

John Wesley Cromwell wrote in 1882, "However much the colored people may be under the bane of proscription, with respect to their social

An undated photo of the interior of the Twelfth Street YMCA building at 1816 Twelfth Street, Northwest. *Library of Congress, Prints & Photographs Division, HABS.*

and political rights, they can at least congratulate themselves…that they are at liberty to spend their money as they choose. And we suggest it is high time to begin discriminating in the matter of our patronage."[196] This separatist philosophy inspired the establishment of uppity clubs like the Bethel Literary and Historical Society, the Mu-So-Lit Society and, with the reputation of the most difficult to join, the exclusive Monocan Club of 1899. An array of elite sororities for women of color, fraternities for Black men, settlement houses, mutual aid societies and mutual benefit associations, as well as charitable and reform clubs, also took shape during the early twentieth century. There remained additional clubs for various groups of the Black community: the Lotus Club, Sparta Club, Manhattan Club and Acanthus Club. Some of these clubs and learning institutions were organized by clergy leaders, since churches supported most aspects of African American life.[197] By 1957, there were 108 religious institutions in the corridor alone,[198] according to a church survey.

Daniel Payne of the Metropolitan African Methodist Episcopal Church founded the Bethel Literary and Historical Association. Francis J. Grimké of the Fifteenth Street Presbyterian Church housed M Street High School in the church's basement. Founded in 1870, M Street High was the nation's first high school for Black youth and had a reputation of excellence. The outstanding school enrolled several prominent Black innovators, including

Howard University Law School graduating class, circa 1900. *Library of Congress, Prints & Photographs Division.*

historian Rayford L. Logan, poet Sterling Brown, diplomat Mercer Cook, army lieutenant colonel West Hamilton, federal judge William H. Hastie and blood plasma researcher Charles H. Drew.[199] Reverend Crummell of Saint Luke's Episcopal Church propelled the development of the first learned Black society in the country, the American Negro Academy. At seventy-eight-years-old, Crummell established the academy in 1897 as "an organization of authors, scholars, artists, and those distinguished in other walks of life, men of African descent, for the promotion of Letters, Science, and Art." Over time, members would include W.E.B. Du Bois, James Weldon Johnson, Carter G. Woodson, Alaine Locke and Archibald Grimké.[200] The Lincoln Temple Business College in Shaw was founded by pharmacist and business activist William H. Davis in the early 1900s after the business colleges in D.C. wouldn't accept Black students.[201] However, skin color wasn't just a discriminatory problem among whites. Churches and schools played a role in creating a color divide between dark-skin and light-skin African Americans, between wealthy and impoverished.

The Black community drew strong class distinctions in Northwest: the elitists of Howard University and LeDroit Park, the working class of Shaw and the blues players and pool hall goers who lived in the alleyways of Seventh Street and U all resided close to one another but were separated based on church, society, income, school and skin tone.[202] Writer John Edward Hasse illustrates the social classes as a pyramid:

> At the top was a small aristocracy, comprising about 60 or 70 families— generally people of light skin color, who themselves or ancestors had lived in Washington for many years, who pursued "honorable occupations," and who had a certain amount of money and education. Next was a middle class of government workers, professionals, and businessmen....The largest and poorest section...comprised recent migrants from the South, many of whom lived lives of destitution and economic deprivation.

Jazz composer and U Street native Duke Ellington recalled the rift growing up: "I don't know how many castes of Negroes there were in the city at the time, but I do know that if you decided to mix carelessly with another, you would be told that one just did not do that sort of thing."[203] But some Washingtonians refused to tolerate colorism and class divisions in the Black community.

Vigorous promoter of self-help Nannie Helen Burroughs worked to level the playing field for low-income, darker-skinned Blacks after struggling to find a job at the end of the nineteenth century. The dark-skinned daughter of former slaves and M Street High mentee of Mary Church Terrell and Anna Julia Cooper excelled in her studies. But when she graduated in 1896, she faced difficulty obtaining a job in the D.C. school system, which she attributed to "politics" that singled out and selected better-connected, lighter-skinned peers. In her 1904 essay "Not Color but Character," exasperated with what she called "colorphobia," she condemned the straightening of hair and wholesale bleaching of faces. She stated, "Color is no badge of superiority of mind nor soul." She also served as the head of the National Baptist Women's Convention and openly opposed lynching, voting restrictions and employment discrimination. In 1909, she opened the National Training School for Women and Girls with thirty-five students on a six-acre hilltop on Fiftieth and Grant Streets Northeast.[204]

Despite color tensions among Blacks and increased separation from whites, the spirit of enterprise continued to manifest in U Street's working class. In 1902, Armstrong Vocational High School opened in the

Portrait of Nannie Helen Burroughs in 1879. *Library of Congress.*

neighborhood, competing with a white technical school built at the same time.[205] Later, Cardozo High School opened in the U Street neighborhood, focusing on business.[206]

A Harlem Renaissance poet activist recalled his time working for Black historian Carter G. Woodson in the mid-1920s:

> *When I worked for Dr. Woodson, he set an example in industry and stick-to-it-tiveness for his entire staff since he himself worked very hard....One never got the idea that the boss would ask you to do anything that he would not do himself. His own working day extended from early morning to late at night....*
>
> *One time Dr. Woodson went away on a trip....He came back on the third day and found us all in the shipping room playing cards. Nobody got fired. Instead he requested our presence in his study where he gave us a long and very serious talk on our responsibilities to our work, to history, and to the Negro race. And he predicted that neither we nor the race would get ahead playing cards during working hours.[207]*

The "stick-to-it-tiveness" and drive to better the Black race that began in the fight for abolition would continue in the fight for civil rights. As Black business boomed, Black ministers preached and Black educators instructed, the battle to end Jim Crow still loomed, and African Americans would have no time to waste in opposing the coming racist policies of the Woodrow Wilson administration. W.E.B. Du Bois's "talented tenth," the chartering of the NAACP's D.C. branch in 1913[208] and Woodson's establishment of Negro History in 1926 would make sure that the "Negro race" would not fail. "The Secret City" had already begun to gain a sense of unity and pride that would become a necessity after World War I, as the election of Wilson to the presidency in 1912 segregated the civil service throughout the nation.[209]

NEW SLAVERY VERSUS NEW NEGRO

It was a time of "New Freedom," according to President Woodrow Wilson's 1912 Democratic vision for a progressive Washington: "Should I become President of the United States, [Negroes] may count upon me for absolute fair dealing and for everything by which I could assist in advancing the interests of their race in the United States."[210] America's twenty-eighth president sang a tune of "fair and just treatment" for all, a promise D.C. Blacks were eager to listen to as segregation in the District had already become a trend.

White antagonism had begun shoving Jim Crow streetcar bills onto the desks of congressmen as early as 1906, while the Black members of the Board of Trade had all resigned, feeling unwelcome. The very first Jim Crow corner appeared in 1904 at the Bureau of Engraving and Printing, and by 1909, segregated lockers, washrooms and lunchroom accommodations were already an enforced rule in several sections of the Treasury and the Department of the Interior. In 1910, white churches excluded their fellow Black Christians from participating in a major convention. That same year, ten Black neighborhood groups were kicked out of the Federation of Citizens' Association, prompting African Americans to form their own civic associations. The *Bee* journaled in 1905, "A systematic effort inaugurated to Jim Crow the Negro. The fever is spreading....The Negro is afraid to complain."

Black Washingtonians may have been spared lynchings, but they were already subject to most of the discriminations imposed on Black people elsewhere in the country prior to Wilson taking office. Republican president

William Taft offered African Americans leadership appointments but turned a blind eye to the segregation already beginning in various parts of the federal government. As a white officer of the NAACP explained about the Wilson administration, "Segregation, is no new thing in Washington, and the present administration cannot be said to have inaugurated it. The past few months of Democratic Party control, however, have given segregation impetus and have been marked by more than a beginning of systematic enforcement."[211] The Virginia-born president may not have initiated Jim Crow in D.C., but his racist legislation was surely to blame for the toppling of Black Washington. What had once been a general practice of racial snubbing and barring became officially sanctioned under the Wilson rule. Early in his presidency, Wilson dismissed all but two of the African American appointments President Taft had granted "to offices of essential dignity at Washington." By 1916, the only Black person to hold an appointive position in the city was Robert Terrell.

Now there was a more militant approach to segregation in the District, and the effects, as the NAACP reported, were "startling." Booker T. Washington, slave-born intellectual and author of the famed 1901 autobiography *Up from Slavery*,[212] described his disheartening visit to the city in 1913: "I have recently spent several days in Washington, and I have never seen the colored people so discouraged and bitter as they were at that time."[213] The moment Wilson took office, a group of "Negro baiters" calling themselves the National Democratic Fair Play Association went on a mission to kick Blacks out of the federal government. The pestilent committee stirred up trouble in the White House, poking around various offices fishing for complaints against Black workers. The members sought to remove Blacks from civil service, restrict them to menial jobs or at least keep workers segregated.

With the backing of the new president and office seekers who thought it intolerable for whites to work in proximity to Blacks, the so-called fairness group got its way. The Treasury, Post Office Department and Navy Department were soon added to the list of segregated federal offices, where lunch tables and bathrooms were divided.[214] Southern Democrats in Congress continued to challenge the District's customs of integration, reintroducing bills to prohibit interracial marriage and going as far as proposing to send all African Americans out of the United States—an idea of Chevy Chase founder Senator Francis Newlands. Black morale in the city declined as Wilson and his appointees clung to southern ideals of white supremacy.

Wilson served as the first southerner elected to the presidency since before the Civil War—a regional reconciliation whites longed for since the

POST-OFFICE, WASHINGTON.

Northeast view of the post office in the 1860s. *Library of Congress.*

Reconstruction era. The former New Jersey governor campaigned on "New Freedom" and progressivism, yet somehow, he and his followers couldn't see how segregation contradicted those promises. So, more "Negro corners" and "colored toilets" appeared throughout federal buildings, and some even erected a few "Whites Only" signs. Wilson defended his approach, claiming forced separation protected Black workers from discrimination and was necessary to avoid racial "friction…discontent and uneasiness." Administrative heads agreed with Wilson, suggesting to critics that Black employees were happier segregated—an attitude resembling antebellum slave masters who insisted slaves were pleased with their condition.

Director of the Bureau of Engraving and Printing Joseph Ralph explained to the wife of Senator Robert La Follette of Wisconsin, Belle, the tables set aside in the back of the lunchroom for employees of color were not a "general order" but better for blacks to associate with one another while eating. "Colored employees have expressed themselves as believing that arrangements of this kind, including separate toilet conveniences, were very satisfactory and proper," Ralph insisted, "and it would seem that the claim of discrimination is made only by colored persons who do not desire to associate with members of their own race." Ralph initially thought a segregated bureau was impractical but was quick to comply with the new orders that came from acting secretary of the treasury John Skeleton Williams in 1913 after Williams spotted white and Black women working side by side and opposite each other at the bureau. Ralph, like other agency officials, took the requests from higher-ups to institute the new policies, and according to Ralph, most Black workers obeyed without complaint.[215]

Questioning the new system was something Blacks were wary of doing, as defiance could cost their jobs. Blacks were already losing their jobs or being demoted to dead-end, out-of-sight positions[216] due to the fair play committee and complaints from white workers. In one instance, Rose Miller, a white woman who worked at the bureau, complained about Louise Nutt, a Black supervisor, and within a week, Ralph replaced Nutt with a white man.

U Street resident Rosebud Murraye was not afraid to speak out against the injustices. The "mulatto" D.C. native, as the census classified her, was active in the U Street community and her church. Murraye had worked her way up to serving as a printer's assistant at the Bureau of Engraving and Printing. She started off in an entry-level position by taking the civil service exam after graduating from Scotia Seminary in North Carolina at the age of nineteen. By time Wilson took office in March 1913, Murraye had been working for the bureau for nine years and wasn't willing to go along with William's new system.

Shortly after Williams's visit to the bureau, she found herself confronting the new policies head on, refusing to sit at lunch tables apart from her white counterparts. Murraye banded together with two other Black printer's assistants, Bertha Saunders and Maggie Keys, to challenge Williams. The women repeatedly defied segregation in the cafeteria, at one point, two employees—one white and one Black—urged them to move tables. Eventually, Ralph called the ladies into his office and had white housing reformer Charlotte Hopkins lecture them about following the rules. The women stood their ground, explaining that there was no separate lunchroom for Blacks, just a waiting area next to the toilets. According to the *Bee*, Hopkins asked, "Why will you go where you are not wanted? Do you know that the Democrats are in power? If you people will go along and behave yourselves and stay away from places where you are not wanted, we may let you hold your places." Murraye still did not back down, or as Ralph described it, she was unwilling to "behave." According to Ralph, Murraye was "impertinent" and "insolent" at the meeting. Though they didn't have the full support of their Black coworkers, the ladies decided to boycott the lunchroom altogether. Thwarted internally, the protestors brought their complaints to the recently founded NAACP.[217]

The D.C. branch of the civil rights organization was founded in March 1912 and chartered on June 3, 1913, as a local version of the national network of activists established in 1909 to combat Jim Crow. D.C.'s chapter was predominantly Black, something that set it apart from the nationwide organization. When Murraye and her comrades connected with the NAACP in the spring of 1913, they received little assistance from the branch's founding president, J. Milton Waldron. Belle La Follete, one of the branch's few white members, and the wife of Senator "Fighting Bob" La Follete, took matters into her own hands.[218] She published the complaints of the three women in *La Follette's Magazine*, now known as the *Progressive*.

Murraye was fired for insubordination shortly after the interview printed, so Belle responded to President Wilson directly. She forwarded Murraye's statements to Wilson, stating in her cover letter that the situation was a concern of "the larger question of human rights." Wilson's secretary denied that the abrupt firing was related to the article. In response, Belle wrote a series of pieces in her magazine about the injustices in the federal civil service. She explained that African Americans "should not be discriminated against and should be accorded the justice due them as citizens of a democracy. What becomes of the fundamental principles of our institutions if the color line or any other arbitrary line can be drawn by the government among its civil service employees?"[219] In the end, Belle helped Murraye find a new job.

Waldron's NAACP presidency was short-lived. The pastor of Shiloh Baptist Church (located at Ninth and P Streets in the historic Shaw district since 1924) was swallowed in political controversy after campaigning for Wilson in 1912. Reverend Waldron was a social advocate who turned sour toward the Republicans after Theodore Roosevelt's treatment of Black soldiers in the Brownsville, Texas riot of 1906. In a postelection speech in Richmond, Waldron told the audience that white southerners were "our best friends in everything except politics." The minister admired Wilson's progressive reforms, although those ideals backfired once Wilson took office and began a segregation binge. Nannie Burroughs and other local critics opposed Waldron's Democratic support, and in the summer of 1913, he was ousted as president. The dissension also pushed some of Shiloh's members to leave the church.[220] One of U Street's key players, Archibald Grimké, replaced Waldron as the D.C. chapter president—a position the lawyer diplomat would hold for the next ten years.

INTERNAL DISCORD

A decade before the start of World War I, America's top Black leaders were at war with one another. The most famous of the leaders, Booker T. Washington, sparked a nationwide debate when he told a racially mixed crowd at the Cotton States and International Exposition in Georgia that Blacks should stay away from political agitation. Washington believed the best route to Black achievement was vocational training and agriculture expertise rather than forcing whites to agree to racial equality. The 1895 speech, later nicknamed the Atlanta Compromise, didn't sit well with Black radicals.

Born a slave in Virginia, Washington prided himself on hard work and self-help. His noble character and work ethic followed him throughout his schooling at Hampton Normal and Agricultural Institute. In 1881, Washington became the leader of the Tuskegee Normal and Industrial Institute, a school that modeled Washington's character.[221] Among white and Black reformers, the Tuskegee Institute held a great rapport, and although some applauded Washington's model of trade training, after his Atlanta speech, Washington's critics became more vocal. Critics viewed his speech as an accommodation to segregation and wanted a more aggressive approach that didn't surrender literary education and, in essence, civil rights. However, Washington believed that if African Americans could prove themselves self-sufficient, then whites would eventually accept Blacks and leave them in peace. In his famous speech, he said, "In all things that are purely social we can be as separate as the fingers, yet one as the hand in all things essential to mutual progress."[222] Washington continued:

> *The wisest among my race understand that the agitation of questions of social equality is the extremist folly, and that progress in the enjoyment of all the privileges that will come to us must be the result of severe and constant struggle rather than of artificial forcing. No race that has anything to contribute to the markets of the world is long in any degree ostracized. It is important and right that all privileges of the law be ours, but it is vastly more important that we be prepared for the exercises of these privileges. The opportunity to earn a dollar in a factory just now is worth infinitely more than the opportunity to spend a dollar in an opera house.[223]*

U Street's Francis Grimké was up for no such compromise. The well-respected pastor of Fifteenth Street Presbyterian Church was one of the first major Black leaders to speak out against the Tuskegee system. From his

Standing portrait of Booker T. Washington in 1917. *Library of Congress.*

U Street pulpit, where the area's elite regularly attended, Francis preached several sermons opposing Booker T. Washington's views. Francis and his brother Archibald were emerging as influential intellectual leaders of Black America. The brothers were familiar with slavery, born to a South Carolina planter and his slave mistress. As Francis expressed his discontent with Booker T. Washington at church, Archibald wrote a series of exchanges to Booker T. Washington while living in Boston. The extended correspondence became a long-distance presentation of competing monologues, with Archibald writing passionately about the rise in lynchings throughout the South and Washington defending his educational philosophy. Although leaders like Francis and Mary Church Terrell had accepted invitations to speak at Tuskegee Institute and even walked away impressed with what they saw, something Terrell would admit years later in her memoir, *A Colored Woman in a White World*, an increase in white aggression was making the noiseless vocational approach seem more and more ineffective.

A split in the leadership of Black America was underway the moment the Grimké brothers openly disagreed with the highly respected philanthropist Booker T. Washington. And embittered whites took advantage of the opportunity. Southern white racists viewed the Atlanta Compromise as a sign of weakness.[224] Booker T. Washington's proposal was an avenue for whites to create a permanent, submissive working class.[225] So, a determination to establish white supremacy multiplied, along with Jim Crow laws. African Americans found themselves limited to education in manual training deemed fit for the subservient workforce.

From Texas through the Gulf states and up to North Carolina, lynchings grew in frequency during the 1890s.[226] The ardor of racial exclusion escalated from segregation to vigilante executions. As author Blair Ruble described the era, it was "turning into a killing season." An average of 100 Americans, the majority Black Americans, were being hanged to death each year throughout the South. In 1892, white mobs hung 161 blacks and 69 whites without a trial. Six years later, inspirited whites viciously overthrew the elected interracial municipal government of Wilmington, North Carolina— still the only successful armed coup in U.S. history.[227] In his farewell speech to Congress in 1901, Representative George White of North Carolina said, "You may tie us and then taunt us for our lack of bravery, but one day we will break the bonds. You may use our labor for two and a half centuries and then taunt us for our poverty, but let me remind you we will not always remain poor." White would be the last man of color to hold a seat in the house for the next thirty years.[228]

The young William Edward Burghardt (W.E.B.) Du Bois was counting on that "one day." A sociologist beyond his years, the Massachusetts native and Harvard graduate responded to Booker T. Washington's conservative ideals with a collection of essays, one in particular titled "Of Mr. Booker T. Washington and Others."[229] The Grimké brothers, having experienced slavery just like Booker T. Washington, were more moderate in their objections and never cut themselves off personally from the Tuskegee leader. Du Bois and leaders like William Monroe Trotter were less restrained and respectful, as they had no personal experience of enslavement. Du Bois spent a summer teaching at Tuskegee University in 1903, until friction between him and Washington led the "double consciousness" writer to break away from Tuskegee.[230]

In Du Bois's 1903 groundbreaking book *The Souls of Black Folks*, the data-driven investigator argued that the race issue was the core challenge of the twentieth century. His sharp critiques strategized an alternative to racial freedom: a pursuit in higher education. Du Bois wanted to rid the country of white tyranny over Black people instead of making accommodations to live among the strife—a criticism of the "Tuskegee machine." With very few options left, the only solution for Blacks to take control of their own lives was to earn an education. The theme of advanced education would continue throughout the twentieth century as people of color learned that knowledge truly possesses power. At this point, the foremost organizations and academic institutions were at odds with one another. The Afro-American Council, the D.C.–based American Negro Academy and the Howard University Board of Regents battled for control of institutional resources. The national discourse had local effects as U Street's elite entangled in the conflict. Black America needed to reconcile sooner than later, so Booker T. Washington took the first step in calling for peace.[231]

In 1903, invitations were sent out to a select few of the era's leaders to attend a conference in New York City's Carnegie Hall. The gathering sought to resolve the public dispute at a private convention. About fifteen Black influencers were invited to attend the conference "representing various sections of the country and various race interests, for the purpose of considering quietly all the weighty matters that now confront us as a race." The meeting was in fact very quiet, as there is little mention of it in earlier histories, and it is only briefly noted in Du Bois's autobiography. The secretive correspondence among invitees leading up to the 1904 meeting showed anti-Tuskegee and pro-Tuskegee groups strategizing and readying their allies. On February 25, 1903, Du Bois sent a letter marked confidential

W.E.B. Du Bois head-and-shoulders portrait, facing slightly right on May 31, 1919. *Library of Congress.*

to U Street's Kelly Miller, the first Black student to be admitted to John Hopkins University.[232] Du Bois wanted to gauge the opinions of the Howard University professor in regards to Booker T. Washington's peace proposal. Du Bois wrote:

> *I was asked to go to Tuskegee some time ago and at that time the Conference you have been invited* [to] *was cooked up. A little judicious pressure and insistence led to your invitation and that of* [C.G.] *Morgan of Cambridge* [Massachusetts]. *I do not now recall all the names but it includes* [J.W.] *Lyons, Bishop Grant, John* [S.] *Trower of Philadelphia, Rev.* [C.T.] *Walker of New York,* [F.L.] *McGhee of St. Paul, etc.*[233]

> *I think this will be a chance for a heart to heart talk with Mr. Washington. I propose to stand on the following platform:*

> *1. Full political rights on the same terms of other Americans.*
> *2. Higher education of selected Negro youth.*
> *3. Industrial education for the masses.*
> *4. Common school training for every Negro child.*
> *5. A stoppage to the campaign of self-depreciation.*
> *6. A careful study of the real conditions of the Negro.*
> *7. A National Negro periodical.*
> *8. A thorough and efficient federation of Negro societies and activities.*
> *9. The raising of a defense fund.*
> *10. A judicious fight in the courts for civil rights.*

> *Finally the general watchword must be, not to put forth dependence on the help of the whites but to organize for self help, encouraging "manliness without defiance, conciliation without servility."*
> *This program is hardly thought out—what is your opinion?*

The list of attendees included Archibald Grimké; Attorney Clement G. Morgan; Washingtonian educator Hugh Browne; Minnesota's first Black lawyer, Frederick L. McGhee; editor T. Thomas Fortune; Washington's chief aide, Emmett J. Scott; Du Bois; and, of course, Booker T. Washington. The gathering lasted three days and ended with the naming of a twelve-member Committee of Safety. The members included Booker T. Washington, Du Bois and Archibald. Archibald negotiated a common strategy that would lead the civil rights movement into the next century. Participants agreed to pursue suffrage, speak out against lynching, formulate a legal defense for filing lawsuits against discriminatory practices and laws, value both industrial and higher education and band together all Americans to resolve racial problems.

Du Bois resigned from the committee shortly after leaving New York. The committee was mostly pro-Tuskegee and was believed to be secretly funded by Andrew Carnegie, so after a second meeting was held at the end of the summer of 1904, though Du Bois was not able to attend due to health reasons and had requested the meeting be postponed, the young leader called it quits. In a letter written several months after his resignation, Du Bois stated, "There was no use trying to cooperate with a man who would act like that.…Whatever I can do to promote harmony I shall do so but I will not put myself under the control and command of Mr. Washington."[234] On July 10, 1905, Du Bois and his comrades met at the Erie Beach Hotel across the Niagara River from Buffalo in Ontario, Canada. Washingtonians Henry L. Baily and W.H.H. Hart were in attendance, along with *Washington Bee* editor Calvin Chase. The Niagara Movement was officially chartered in D.C., meeting a second time in Harper's Ferry in August 1906.

At the same time, the area's community leaders were becoming fed up with widespread outbreaks of racism. From the national 1906 Brownsville riots by whites against Black soldiers wrongly accused of shooting a white police officer and bartender to the local appointment of Howard University's white, racist president John Gordon, U Street's moderate leaders found themselves taking a more radical stance. Not only was discrimination on the rise, but it had also arrived on U Street's doorstep. Protests against Gordon turned into a student uprising that was brutally quashed by the District's all-white police force.[235]

At the time, Francis Grimké was serving as a university trustee. Archibald was also living in D.C. with his daughter, Angelina Weld Grimké, a schoolteacher at U Street's Armstrong Manual Training School and later at Dunbar High School. While teaching, she wrote a play about lynching. *Rachel* was the first full-length play written, produced and performed by Blacks in the twentieth century. The NAACP's Drama Committee produced it in 1916.[236] Archibald published his most influential work, "The Heart of the Race Problem," around the Niagara Movement's second meeting.[237] Archibald argued that the propensity of white men to rape women of color was at the root of American racism, a topic Archibald explored as a product of mixed racial ancestry.[238]

This photograph created in 1905 shows a group of the founding members of the Niagara Movement superimposed over an image showing Niagara Falls in the background. *Library of Congress, Prints and Photographs Division.*

U Street's leaders were searching for answers. They were writing essays, hosting rallies and forming civil groups, but the nation was still in need of change—of massive unification. So, in 1909, despite Washington already having the National Negro Suffrage League and the Negro Personal Liberty Party, a group of interracial liberals banded together to form one political, civil powerhouse, the NAACP.[239]

NAACP

The Niagara Movement disbanded after voting to establish the NAACP under the leadership of W.E.B. Du Bois, Archibald Grimké, Oswald Garrison Villard, William English Walling, Henry Moskowitz, Mary White Ovington and Ida Wells-Barnett. The organization was headquartered in New York. The NAACP D.C. chapter became the most influential branch in the nation. The District branch had the advantage of being located near federal lawmakers as well as a large base of middle-class supporters. Thus a power struggle over control of the Washington chapter was imminent. Aside from the internal battle of power between headquarters and the District chapter, Washington's prosperous African American community wanted local leadership to be in the hands of the professional class and away from religious politicians. This led to Archibald Grimké replacing Reverend Waldron as the president of the D.C. chapter only a year into its establishment. The headquarters versus local battle continued until a 1942 court case resolved the Washington chapter as subordinate to the national organization. For at least the first ten years of the D.C. chapter's functioning, Archibald turned it into the largest and strongest branches.[240]

Archibald was born in 1849, one of three mixed-race sons. He attended Lincoln University in Pennsylvania and later became the second Black graduate of Harvard Law School. He served as U.S. consul to Santo Domingo from 1894 to 1898. The nephew of Angelina and Sarah Grimké, arguably the most important white southern abolitionists in the antebellum era, Archibald seized on the matter of segregation in the federal government as D.C.'s NAACP headman. A columnist for the *New York Daily Age* and president of the American Negro Academy, Archibald rejected white supremacy with independence and vigor. Kelly Miller described the snow-white-haired man as "a radical among radicals." Within months, the D.C.

branch surged in membership as Archibald pressed to collect the District's disagreeable community behind the local NAACP. Membership grew from 143 to 700 participants. Under his leadership, the local organization planned and executed a series of protests and mass meetings. In October 1913, a rally was hosted a mile from U Street, just five blocks from the White House at Metropolitan A.M.E. Church. The NAACP–coordinated meeting attracted an overflow crowd of nearly 10,000 congregants.[241] The Metropolitan A.M.E. has more than 175 years of history and still stands in its original location not too far from U Street.[242]

Blacks all over the country were taking a stand against President Wilson's discriminatory policies. As the editors of the weekly Black newspaper *Independent* described in November 1913, the District of Columbia had no distinction between races since the equal rights amendments were passed, and now, forty years later, the Wilson administration was changing everything:

> *There had been no trouble these forty years, not even under Democratic administrations, but now the colored clerks, men and women, are to be kept separate, as unfit to mingle on even terms in the business of Government.... Think how self-respecting colored employees, gentlemen and ladies, do feel mortified and indignant.*
>
> *In various bureaus colored women have been put in rooms by themselves; colored men have been treated in the same way and there are dressing rooms labeled "For Colored Women."*
>
> *The negro deputation to visit the President well says that segregation cannot be justified, but "is calculated and intended to stamp colored citizens with a badge of indignity, making the menials and inferiors in the house of a Government that knows no racial distinctions among all its citizens." It is not patriotic, it is not democratic.*[243]

Nationally, Washington was on the brink of a racial upset. Internationally, Washington was contending for global recognition. Archibald and fellow African American leaders played on the city's new federal platform, promoting foreign affairs to draw attention to the local injustices happening behind the idealistic front Wilson was projecting to the world. Still, the NAACP's advocacy was not enough to halt segregation in the federal workforce. Wilson's administration deliberately placed limitations on Black advancement. Throughout the president's two terms, white administrators denied well-qualified Black applicants job opportunities, filed negative personnel reports about employees of color and declined promotions to

African American veterans. In 1914, an executive order was issued to easily identify the race of federal applicants, making it easier to discriminate against Blacks. The order required applicants to include a photograph with their applications, and a number of agencies required personal interviews. The increased discrimination directly affected the middle-class U Streeters.

John Abraham Davis, for instance, was a D.C. native and valedictorian of M Street High School. The mulatto man began a career at the Government Printing Office in 1882. Over the years, Davis, described by a supervisor as "thorough and energetic," went from making $0.25 an hour as a low-level laborer to earning a $1,400.00 salary as a white-collar clerk. Davis supervised a staff of ten workers, nine of whom were white. His family lived in a nice home on S Street, Northwest, and an eighty-five-acre farm in rural Virginia. A month after Wilson's inauguration in March 1913, Davis was demoted, and his salary experienced a 15 percent cut. The following year, Davis was relegated to the laborer position that he entered the printing office with three decades earlier, making $500.00 a year. Despite Davis's outcry, his federal wages were lowered, and his family sank into poverty.[244]

Wilson was snatching jobs away from the very group of people who helped put him in office, wiping away Black people's financial security and ultimately crippling Black migration to D.C.[245] Observers speculate that Wilson may have won more Black votes than any other Democratic candidate had ever received. Du Bois wrote that Wilson championed the votes of more than 100,000 African Americans in the North alone.[246] Now, the Black supporters who Wilson had deceived were feeling the weight of the president's empty promises and strategic racist policies. By 1920, barely 25 percent of the District's inhabitants were Black—the lowest population since before the Civil War.[247]

RED SUMMER, 1919

In 1914, a European war was underway. The Great War, later known as World War I, resulted in more than 16 million people dead worldwide by the end of the four-year conflict that pit the globe's central powers and allied powers against one another. What began as a spar for nationalism between Serbia and Austria-Hungary, escalated to Germany, Austria-Hungary, Bulgaria and the Ottoman Empire militarizing against Great Britain, France, Russia, Italy, Romania, Japan and, in 1917, the United States. In February

1917, Congress passed a $250 million arms appropriations bill to prepare the America for war. Soon after, Germany sunk four U.S. commercial ships. On April 2, 1917, President Wilson declared war on Germany before the members of Congress.[248]

For white Washington, the war attracted an influx of Deep South migrants. In addition to an expansion in American armed forces, the federal government was in need of fresh workers as new agencies were created to support the war effort. Women went to work by the numbers in low-level agency occupations such as clerks, bookkeepers and stenographers, while their male counterparts went off to battle. An estimated sixty to seventy-five thousand new laborers arrived in the city in the first few months of American's participation in the war. For Black Washington, this meant a slowing of Black migration, as white newcomers quickly adapted to the District's racial customs, taking over jobs and refusing to live in Black neighborhoods. Wilson's bureaucracy remained intact during the war, although rigid separation was unintentionally going unnoticed as the international crisis caused economic hardships in the capital. The defense for world democracy inspired Blacks to push for their own freedom on the home front. World War I gave men of color a chance to prove themselves as equal. Blacks wanted full citizenship, and what better way to dismantle Jim Crow than volunteering to protect the safety of democracy.

Local churches and organizations rallied Black men to register for the draft. The First Separate Battalion of the D.C. National Guard, 50 officers and 929 enlisters, took up posts to guard the White House,[249] power plants and reservoirs around the city and were among the first soldiers to be called into service. The Black regiment was later renamed the 372nd Infantry.[250]

Several thousand Black men registered for the draft, but discrimination in the military remained. For instance, M Street High alumnus Rayford Logan served as an officer in the 372nd, but after his duty at combat, he resided in France for several years, not wanting to return home to discrimination in D.C. Another U Streeter and M Street graduate Charles Hamilton Houston experienced negativity while serving in the war, fueling him to become a civil rights litigator. He is now applauded as the "Man Who Killed Jim Crow." America's army initially excluded Black soldiers from combat, instead they were given jobs as cooks and cleaners.

U Street leaders Archibald Grimké and Kelly Miller met with Secretary of War Newton Baker to negotiate for integrated military camps where Black recruits would be trained for battle. Miller and Archibald, along with their colleagues in attendance at the meeting, recognized that African

Americans needed an opportunity to fully participate in the war effort if they were going to show the country that Blacks were not second-rate citizens. Baker agreed to segregated military training camps, which was not the preferred response, but at least Black soldiers could now demonstrate their skill on the battle lines. "There need not be the slightest apprehension concerning [the Black man's] loyalty, soldierly efficiency or willingness to serve his country....Those who fight for the honor and glory of the flag are worthy of a full measure of freedom and privilege under that flag," Miller told the *Evening Star* in 1917.[251]

When Black fighters arrived home from World War I, they returned to a country still unwilling to share freedom and privilege on the basis of skin tone. The praise and honor soldiers of color experienced overseas for defending democracy alongside foreign comrades was very different from the welcome war veterans received when they marched back onto U.S. soil. The racist policies of Wilson were still in effect, discrimination was still at large and, concerned that Black veterans had returned with a new self-confidence, white people were even more threatened by the idea of Black progression.

Their suspicions proved true. America's Black defenders were awakened by their experiences abroad.[252] Archibald described the Black soldier: "[He] has come back not as he went but a New Negro. He has come back to challenge injustice in his own land and to fight wrong with courage that will not fail him in the bitter and perhaps bloody years to come."[253] The increase in gusto among Black people to fight for their rights didn't fare well with white counterparts.

To add to the tension, Washington's population had swelled to 455,000, about 100,000 more people than at the start of the war. The District was financially strained postwar, and many veterans, white and Black, came home to recession and unemployment. America as a whole was at a tipping point. In 1919, violent attacks by whites against Blacks broke out in a number of American cities. Charleston, South Carolina; Knoxville, Tennessee; Omaha, Nebraska; Philadelphia, Pennsylvania; and Chicago all experienced racially provoked bloodshed in the "Red Summer" of 1919, and on July 18, the race war showed up on U Street's doorstep.[254]

A month before white vigilantes stormed the U Street corridor beating Black residents, there was an alleged series of street crimes and attacks on women by a Black man. As police rounded up suspects and enraged white posses went on "negro hunts," the local press began to print sensationalized stories about the assaults on white women, although the first victim was a Black teacher. Tensions increased as white servicemen roamed the city for the unknown Black perpetrator. According to news coverage of the citizen searches for the "D.C. fiend," heavily armed bands of white men and groups of white-hooded figures were patrolling the neighborhoods at night, stopping and questioning African Americans. Fears of a race riot were on the rise as Washington's newspapers continued to publish racially inflammatory stories of the incidents. The headlines from the city's white daily papers, the *Washington Post*, the *Washington Times*, the *Washington Herald* and the *Evening Star*, read: "13 Suspects Arrested in Negro Hunt"; "Posses Keep Up Hunt for Negro"; "Hunt Colored Assailant"; "Negro Fiend Sought Anew"; and "Negroes Attack Girl, White Men Vainly Pursue."[255] Worried that the District's racially biased press was sowing seeds of animosity and hatred into an already racially strained atmosphere, D.C.'s NAACP wrote a letter to the editors of the four major newspapers in early July, warning them that they were fueling a race riot. But the damage was already done, and the brewing race riot came to full steam at 10:00 p.m. on Friday, July 18.

Twenty-two-year-old Elsie Williams was walking home from her job at the Bureau of Engraving and Printing when two Black men reportedly approached her and tried to steal her umbrella. News of the Southwest D.C. incident caused an explosion of white vengeance. Although Williams was unharmed, the white woman was married to a navy aviation employee, so word of the crime quickly spread throughout the military community. The following night, several hundred "mobbists," as news media called them—mostly soldiers, some in uniform—stormed into the Southwest neighborhood of Bloodfield and attacked several Black residents. The mob was met with little resistance from the police, and no arrests were made the first night of mayhem. On Sunday night, the group grew larger and fiercer, despite the NAACP asking navy secretary Josephus Daniels to restrain the sailors and marines.

The crowd ran rampant throughout downtown and along Pennsylvania Avenue, carrying guns, knives, clubs and rock-filled handkerchiefs. Carter G. Woodson witnessed the terror of that night walking along Pennsylvania Avenue. He recalled, "They had caught a Negro and deliberately held him as one would a beef for slaughter, and when they had conveniently adjusted him for lynching, they shot him. I heard him groaning in his struggle as I hurried away as fast as I could without running, expecting every moment to be lynched myself." City authorities failed to prevent or tame the violence. Two Blacks were beaten in front of the White House, Black riders were dragged off streetcars and pummeled at New York Avenue and Ninth Street, Northwest, and white menaces drove through Black neighborhoods firing gunshots.

On Monday, the *Washington Post* published a front-page story calling for a citywide "clean-up," which many observers have singled out as the principal cause of the riot's escalation. The article, "Mobilization for Tonight," told readers:

> *It was learned that the mobilization of every available service man stationed in or near Washington or on leave here has been ordered for tomorrow evening near the Knights of Columbus hut, on Pennsylvania Avenue between Seventh and Eighth Streets. The hour of assembly is 9 o'clock and the purpose is a "clean-up" that will cause the events of the last two evenings to pale into insignificance.*

The call to arms was intended for the white community, but the Black community heard the warning loud and clear. Black residents, particularly veterans, organized to protect their neighborhoods. Some Black men traveled to Baltimore to purchase firearms because local gun dealers refused to sell to African Americans. Light-skinned war veterans infiltrated white militant groups to collect intelligence, snipers stationed themselves atop row houses, Howard University ROTC officers distributed weapons and ammunition and armed African Americans patrolled U Street between Sixth and Fourteenth Streets, Northwest. Blacks banded together to retaliate against whites, and by the end of the night, it was the deadliest day of the four-day riot. Secretary Baker ordered reinforcements to the city, and Police Chief Raymond Pullman called a guard of four hundred men to cordon off downtown. The violence continued into the next day, and on the final night of the riots, Tuesday, July 22, 1919, President Wilson, who had been on a Potomac River cruise when the situation began, dispatched about two thousand troops to extirpate the madness. The federal cavalry was able to reestablish order to the city with the help of heavy rain. About thirty people died in the four-day race war, scores were wounded and hundreds—less than a dozen white—were detained.[256]

What should've crushed the morale of Black U Street actually brought about a fresh sense of pride and strength. "We are dealing with a new negro and not a slave," Reverend Milton preached at Shiloh Baptist Church the Sunday after the riot.

NAACP's James Weldon Johnson reflected on the bravery of Black Washingtonians in the organization's journal, *Crisis*, stating, "The Negroes saved themselves and saved Washington by their determination not to run but to fight—fight in defense of their lives and their homes." Physically wounded but not spiritually broken, the U Street community rebuilt their neighborhood, worked to exonerate Black detainees, held press conferences and hosted public rallies to defend the reputation of the area's African Americans.[257] The NAACP had a membership of about ten thousand, but shortly after the war, in 1919, membership skyrocketed to eighty thousand. Entering 1920, the corridor was on the brink of an economic revival. Intellectuals, artists, playwrights, lawyers, singers, poets, money-makers, medical scholars, historians and fearless activists had already begun to settle in what would be known in a few years as Black Broadway. Greater U Street would never be the same.

6

YOU STREET

Everybody knew everybody. We didn't miss going downtown. We didn't give a shit. I mean, excuse my language, but they wanted to have all that stuff to themselves, fine—we had all this stuff to ourselves.
—Richard Lee, second-generation owner of Lee's Flower & Card Shop at 928 U Street, open since 1945[258]

Before the twenty-first century's Shinola and luxury high-rises, there was Black Broadway. It was the Roaring Twenties, and the U Street corridor was home to more than three hundred black-owned businesses, around one hundred churches and an array of after-hours spots. The electric nightlife and theaters championed the corridor as "Black Broadway" during the 1930s and 1940s, in reference to New York's popular theater district, Broadway.[259] With Howard University as the greater U Street hub to the east, the corridor stretched for a dozen blocks to Sixteenth Street on the west. U Street was the core of commercial activity, but the community encompassed S, T, V and Fourteenth Streets, as well as some parts of Florida Avenue.[260] In other parts of town, Blacks were still subject to Jim Crow laws, despite the end of Wilson's presidency. But on U Street, African Americans inspired by leaders like Howard professor Alaine Locke and newly appointed D.C. NAACP president Neval Thomas, were free to embrace the emerging New Negro Renaissance.

A new cultural movement had begun nationwide after World War I and the 1919 riots. The economy was booming. Fortunately for U Street, the segregation around the District pushed Blacks to own their own enterprises, something that was possible for people of color along the corridor.[261]

So, the "city within a city" was flooded with unsegregated concert halls and nightclubs that hosted around-the-clock performances by the likes of Pearl Bailey, Cab Calloway and Sarah Vaughan. During the mid-1920s, the Republic Theater at Fourteenth and U, the Lincoln at Thirteenth and U and the Dunbar at Seventh and T sold nearly 1.4 million tickets a year.[262] Black-owned pharmacies, barbershops, pool halls, funeral homes and hotels patronized by African Americans—and funded with loans from Black financiers like the city's oldest Black-owned bank, Industrial Savings—flourished. Black Washingtonians sent their kids to day camp at the country's first African American YMCA, worshipped together in scores of neighborhood churches like Shaw's Lincoln Congregational Temple and launched a movement against segregation from Black Broadway's many gathering places, protesting "don't buy where you can't work."

By the 1960s, the area had birthed some of America's most influential Black leaders and intellectuals—the great jazz band leader and pianist Duke Ellington and the world's first renowned Black opera singer, Madame Lillian Evanti; the pioneering Dr. Charles Drew, who created the country's first blood bank; and lawyer and Howard University professor Charles Hamilton Houston, whose famed student Thurgood Marshall prevailed in *Brown vs. Board of Education*.

The following is a photographic look at the vibrant U Street corridor in those heady days before desegregation and the 1968 riots transformed "You" Street.

EDUCATION

I remember in 1954—May 17, 1954, the principal, Charles Lofton sounded the buzzer whenever you have an announcement, you have a little ding dong and he said, "I wanted to tell you something that"—I don't remember his exact words—"that is of great importance to our city and our country, and that is the Supreme Court of the United States has just declared that schools that are segregated like Dunbar should be unconstitutional." I remember distinctly teachers crying, and it was a very historic day.

And Dunbar of course is a very historic institution. Dunbar graduates went to all the Ivy League schools. It was the only college preparatory high school in the District of Columbia. You didn't have to take a test to get in there. But it was the only college preparatory high school, except for Spingarn, which was relatively new. So, it has a storied history of all of these African Americans who, [like] Charles Drew, graduated of course.[263]

—Congresswoman Eleanor Holmes Norton, a delegate from the District of Columbia, native Washingtonian, civil rights leader and Dunbar High graduate.

M Street High School, located at M Street between New Jersey Avenue and First Street, Northwest, is now the Perry School Community Services Center. The nonprofit provides services for the area's impoverished people with the focuses of youth development and social and economic empowerment. In 1870, M Street High School began as the Preparatory High School for Negro Youth, the first public high school for Black students in the United States. The school opened in the basement of the Fifteenth Street Presbyterian Church, and after moving twice, the school settled and officially opened in 1891. The school would later be renamed Dunbar High School, as its pictured above, in 1943. *Library of Congress, Prints & Photographs Division, Farm Security Administration/Office of War Information Black-and-White Negatives.*

Students working in a machine shop at the Armstrong Technical High School, located at O Street between First and Second Streets, Northwest, in March 1942. The school was built between 1900 and 1902. Originally called Armstrong Manual Training School, in honor of General Samuel Chapel Armstrong, the site was designed by local architect Waddy B. Wood, and it specialized in vocational training. The twenty-eight-room building was designed for 300 students. By the 1950s, after renovations, the school accommodated nearly 1,300 students. The historic site is now the Friendship Armstrong Academy, a public charter school.[264] *Library of Congress, Prints and Photographs Division.*

A portrait of poet Paul Laurence Dunbar. In 1916, M Street High School was renamed Dunbar High School after the first nationally recognized Black poet. The school was known as the best African American high school in America, until school integration in 1955. Dunbar attracted teachers with outstanding credentials because most colleges at the time did not hire Black professors, so the students were educated with an advanced curriculum by the nation's top Black scholars, including Carter G. Woodson, Dr. Charles Drew, Georgiana Simpson and Anna Julia Cooper.[265] *Library of Congress.*

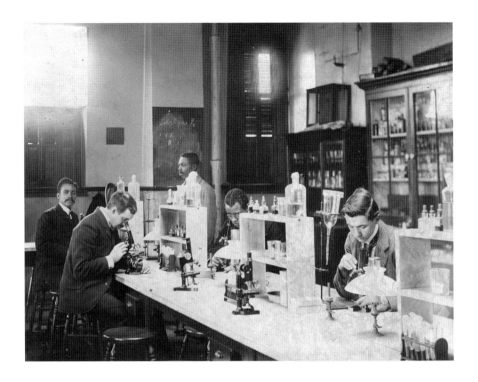

Black and white students working in the bacteriology laboratory at Howard University in 1900. Named after Civil War hero General Oliver O. Howard, Howard University opened in 1867 as one of the first institutions to accept African American students. The university functioned as the heart of U Street, producing world-renowned achievers, such as publisher of the *Afro-American* newspaper Carl Murphy, psychologist Kenneth B. Clark, historian Rayford Logan, photographer Gordon Parks, nurse Mabel Keaton Staupers, Atlanta mayor and United Nations ambassador Andrew Young and the first person of color to receive the Nobel Peace Prize, Ralph Bunche. The college also fostered social civic groups, sports teams, fraternities and even beauty pageants.[266] *Library of Congress, Prints and Photographs Division.*

Opposite: The cover of Carter G. Woodson's textbook recording the history of African Americans. Woodson was born in Buckingham County, Virginia, to the parents of former slaves. After becoming the second Black American to earn a doctorate in history—DuBois being the first—Woodson dedicated his life to digging up African American history. His Harvard University advisers argued that Blacks had no history, but Woodson sought to prove otherwise. Woodson moved to D.C., where he taught various subjects at

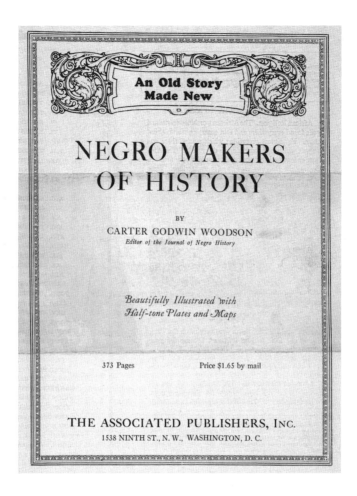

M Street High School, including French and Spanish, and served as the principal of Armstrong Manual Training School. In 1915, he established the Association for the Study of Negro Life and History in collaboration with Jesse E. Moorland. They published the *Journal of Negro History*. The association opened an office on U Street and held seminars and lectures at the nearby Twelfth Street YMCA and YWCA. Folklorist Zora Neale Hurston worked for him at one time, as did historian Rayford Logan. In 1926, the historic explorer established Negro History Week during the second week of February to correspond with the birthdays of Frederick Douglass and Abraham Lincoln. In 1976, the week expanded into a month-long commemoration still celebrated today as Black History Month during February.[267] *Library of Congress.*

WORSHIP

[When asked what makes U Street special.] *Legacy. The Street that the church is on is named after my dad.*[268]

—Kevin Hart, second-generation pastor of the Christian Tabernacle Church, which has stood at 2033 Eleventh Street since 1986

An 1899 photograph of the former building of Fifteenth Street Presbyterian Church. In 1841, the church was opened by John F. Cook Sr., the District's first Black Presbyterian minister. The original location of the church was organized in a frame schoolhouse on Fifteenth Street between I and K Streets. During the late 1800s, one of Cook's sons, George F.T. Cook, was appointed as the superintendent of the Colored Public Schools of Washington and Georgetown. During the Black Broadway era, the church relocated to the U Street neighborhood on Fifteenth and R Streets, Northwest.[269] *Library of Congress, Prints and Photographs Division.*

The interior, looking northeast, of St. Luke's Episcopal Church at Fifteenth and Church Streets, Northwest. The church was the first independent Black Episcopal church in Washington. The ministry was established in 1873 by Reverend Alexander Crummell, an impassioned orator who started the church for "colored" people as a breakaway church from white Episcopalians. Construction of the church began with an initial congregant contribution amount of $650.[270] The church is still open today. *Library of Congress, Prints and Photographs Division.*

The United House of Prayer for All People at 601 M Street, Northwest in 1943. The church was founded in Harlem, New York, in the 1920s by Bishop C.M. Grace, better known as "Sweet Daddy" Grace. Many Black Washingtonians remember him for his flashy dress, long colorful fingernails and flamboyant personality. Grace once baptized 208 converts with water provided by special D.C. fire company equipment in the center of M Street in front of a crowd of 15,000 onlookers. By 1960, the ministry had locations in fourteen states across the country.[271] The ministry is still functioning today. *Library of Congress, Prints and Photographs Division.*

Vermont Avenue Baptist Church pictured in 1899. The church was formed as the Fifth Street Baptist Church in 1866 by former slaves who had been attending Nineteenth Street Baptist Church. They were led by Reverend John H. Brooks. The church has been an integral part of U Street's Black community from its beginning. The ministry was one of Industrial Bank's first shareholders. More than a century old, the church is still open today.[272] *Library of Congress, Prints and Photographs Division.*

COMMUNITY

I think that when you go back to the pre-integration or during the era of segregation, women had a place, and that place was in the home. That place was by your partner, by your husband, taking care of the children. But I think the Phyllis Wheatley YWCA afforded a new venue for the women. I think it provided them with an opportunity to really have a voice and to be heard, and when I examined the early history of the Y, I was amazed at what these extraordinary women could do and how they made a difference in the community beyond their mere household duties, and I remember reading where the wife of [Senator] Blanche K. Bruce was a very well-noted club woman. She was a housewife as well, helped to organize the Book Lovers club prior to the Y even being organized. So, she was one of the earlier members of that book club back in the late nineteenth century, and she helped to found the Phyllis Wheatley YWCA.

Initially, it was called the Colored YWCA before it became the Phyllis Wheatley YWCA, and when I say they had a voice, there were times when you could not do something singley, but when you were with a group of strong ladies, you felt bold. You felt empowered to do certain kinds of things, and I can remember that there was a situation on Georgia Avenue, Seventh Street, where they were going to open the movies on Sundays, and there were parents and friends who said they didn't want their children going to the movies on Sundays, but the entrepreneurs said, you know we're going to go forward, but I understand that the ladies at the Y, along with some other concerned citizens, were able to march and bounce down the Sunday movies. So, for a long while, young people could not attend movies on Sundays. They had to go to church instead.[273]

—*Dr. Judith A. Webb, historian for the Historic Phyllis Wheatley YWCA*

Opposite, top: Mary McLeod Bethune, founding president of the National Council of Negro Women, visits the Phyllis Wheatley YWCA on Rhode Island Avenue in July 1943. The center was established in 1905 by Black women and was named after Phyllis Wheatley, an enslaved woman and famous nineteenth-century poet. The YWCA moved between facilities before settling on Rhode Island Avenue in 1920, where it stands today. It served as a gathering place for the Shaw neighborhood, welcoming U Street moguls like Carter G. Woodson, who used to take his lunch breaks in the cafeteria. With educational programs, recreational activities, meals for underprivileged children and a shelter for Black southern migrants, the women-led center was a support system for those burdened by segregation and war. *Library of Congress, Prints & Photographs Division, Farm Security Administration/Office of War Information Black-and-White Negatives.*

Bottom: Dr. Mordecai Wyatt Johnson, president of Howard University, in 1938. Johnson served as the first Black president of Howard. Under his leadership, the university was transformed into a premier center for higher education, giving birth to those who reshaped U Street into Black Broadway. The Tennessee-born educator developed a passion for helping the poor and afflicted at a young age, and he used his position as the head of Howard to do just that. "I want my country to conquer all the inhibitions connected with blackness and all of the fears connected with blackness, but I want the original blackness there, and I want this blackness to be unashamed and unafraid," Johnson said in his 1927 induction speech. During his tenure, the faculty grew from 200 to 600, and student enrollment grew from 2,500 to 6,500.[274] *Library of Congress, Prints and Photographs Division.*

Elder Lightfoot Solomon Michaux holding a baby and greeting patrons at his Happy News Cafe on 1727 Seventh Street, Northwest, in 1937. The church-run café was a neighborhood soup kitchen. In 1934, the café served a quarter of a million meals for a penny per plate. Michaux was a major contributor to the city as the founder of the Church of God. The evangelist organized mass baptisms in Griffith Stadium, in one instance bringing in water from the River Jordan; broadcasted *Happy Am I* radio program on CBS Radio Network; and helped keep places like the Howard Theatre open for business by holding worship services there.[275] *Library of Congress, Prints and Photographs Division.*

Opposite: The west façade of the True Reformer Building at 1200 U Street, Northwest. In 1903, the United Order of True Reformers, a Richmond-based Black fraternal benevolent society that served as a bank and insurance company for the Black community, constructed True Reformers Hall. The $60,000 property designed by the city's first Black registered architect, John Anderson Lankford, paved the way for U Street to be a main street for Black Washingtonians. The hall was a source of pride for African Americans, serving as the central location for social and business activity. The founders

built it with the intentions of contributing "to the credit of the Negro race." The dedication ceremony of the gray-brick and limestone-trimmed building welcomed 100,000 attendees. The *Washington Post* headline describing the July 15, 1903 dedication read, "Erected by Negroes, White Race Had No Hand in Any Part of Work." The hall housed an array of lodgeroom, retail and entertainment establishments. In the building was the Colored Business Centre, Chapman's Tailoring and Designing School, a pharmacy and the Silver Slipper Club. The basement contained a drill room for the First Separate Battalion, the District's Black national guard. In 1937, the hall was converted into a gymnasium to make room for the Metropolitan Police Boys Club no. 2—the only one in the city to admit Black children. Within three months of the club's launch, 4,100 youngsters were enrolled in the program. Now, the building is the Public Welfare Foundation.[276] *Library of Congress, Prints and Photographs Division.*

A group of Black war workers are pictured leaving the United Service Organization (USO) branch of the Young Men's Christian Association in D.C. in 1943. During World War II, the YWCA and YMCA, along with four other organizations, banded together to form the USO to aid the men and women of the armed forces in educational and spiritual welfare.[277] The Anthony Bowen YMCA opened in 1853 as the first Y for African American boys. The Twelfth Street branch opened in 1912. The recreational center provided a meeting space for civil rights activists like Supreme Court justice Thurgood Marshall, a sports and swimming day camp for athletes like NBA legend Elgin Baylor and shelter for poet Langston Hughes when he was working as a busboy at Wardman Park Hotel. Today, the building is the Thurgood Marshall Center for Service and Heritage.[278] *Library of Congress, Prints & Photographs Division, Farm Security Administration/Office of War Information Black-and-White Negatives.*

BUSINESS

[Segregation] *kept us all in the same community, and it kept us all patronizing our own businesses…We learned to get along within our own community and to produce and provide everything we needed and because of that the community flourished everybody cared for other people in the community and provided for people in the community, and because the money stayed in the community we were able to build wealth and flourish from a financial standpoint. You know churches and banks were always the hearts the linchpins of these African American communities all across the country.*[279]

—*B. Doyle Mitchell Jr., whose grandfather founded*
Industrial Bank in 1934

A newspaper clipping from the *Afro-American* newspaper on August 20, 1938. Industrial Bank of Washington started in 1934 as the only Black bank in the nation's capital. It began as Industrial

Savings Bank in 1913, but after the Great Depression, the bank closed. Jesse Homer Mitchell, a twenty-one-year-old Howard University student, received a charter from Congress and reopened the financial institution at the bank at Eleventh and U Streets. The bank granted U Street residents car, mortgage and small business loans. Today the bank is one of U Street's three surviving Black family-owned businesses from the Black Broadway era.[280] The other two are Ben's Chili Bowl and Lee's Flower & Card Shop. Afro-American *newspaper.*

(*Left to right*): Kristie Lee, Winnifred Lee and Stacie Lee Banks of Lee's Flower & Card Shop. Lee's Flower & Card Shop came to fruition in 1945 at 928 U Street. William P. Lee moved to D.C. after being a Pullman porter in Montreal, Canada, for seventeen years. He went into the flower business with his brother on Georgia Avenue and W Street, but after a dispute, Lee and his wife, Winnifred, decided to run their own operation. The flower shop was a staple of U Street during Black Broadway, and 80 percent of their patrons were the area's Black-owned funeral homes. The shop also crafted arrangements during football season for Howard's annual Capital Classic, which featured a football game between two Black colleges, a dance and parties, a beauty pageant (Miss Capital Classic) and a parade down U Street. Apart from being florists, Winnifred and William participated in a variety of entrepreneurships. William worked with A. Philip Randolph on the Brotherhood of Sleeping Car Porters union and the American Federation of Labor and Congress of Industrial Organizations (AFL-CIO) and started a group called Northwest Security Investors Inc., which gave second trust loans to Blacks, and Winnifred used to design flowers at the White House. The flower shop is currently located at 1026 U Street, and the ownership has been passed down to the third generation, owned and managed by William and Winnifred's granddaughters, Stacie Lee Banks and Kristi Lee.[281] *Lee's Flower and Card Shop.*

The Whitelaw Apartment House at 1839 Thirteenth Street, Northwest. Entrepreneur and financier John Whitelaw Lewis built the Whitelaw Hotel in 1919 at a cost of more than $100,000. The Italian Renaissance Revival–style building housed some of U Street's greats, including Duke Ellington, who boarded at the upscale hotel in 1935. Race-based exclusion laws prohibited African Americans from booking rooms at luxury hotels, so men and women dined and boarded at the Whitelaw Hotel instead. Guests arrived in their best gowns and suits for social gatherings and formal parties in the hotel's public spaces. To construct the hotel, Lewis organized a stock company, the Whitelaw Apartment House Company, to raise the necessary money. According to the *Washington Bee*, Lewis stressed that he did not want whites to invest in the company but instead wanted Blacks to "so when this prosperity…passes, they can see buildings towering skyward and say to the world 'this is what we have gotten out of prosperity,'" according to an October 5, 1918 article.[282] *Library of Congress, Prints and Photographs Division.*

Ben's Chili Bowl photographed in 1980. The nationally acclaimed restaurant known for its chili half smokes has attracted celebrities, presidents, tourists and U Streeters to its dining room since Ben and Virginia Ali founded the bowl in 1958. Born in Trinidad, Ben came to D.C. from Nebraska to attend Howard's dental school in the 1900s. Ben met Virginia, who had moved from Tappahannock, Virginia, at the age of twenty-one to live with her aunt off Fourteenth Street. She worked at Industrial Bank as a teller. In 1958, they wed, and after hearing that the pool hall at 1213 U Street was closing, the two thought Ben's Chili Bowl would be the perfect place to take its spot. The couple leased the property from Harry Beckley, one of the first Black detectives in Washington and used $5,000 to renovate the space into a restaurant.[283] *Library of Congress, Prints and Photographs Division.*

A crowd of people lined up in front of People's Drug Store off Fourteenth Street, Northwest, in 1920. Although there was a number of prominent Black-owned businesses along the corridor, there remained white-owned businesses, some of which refused to hire Black workers. The Great Depression brought about company closures and employee layoffs, and the first to go were usually African Americans. Blacks could patronize these prejudiced establishments, like the People's at Fourteenth and U, but they certainly could not be hired. A young Dunbar High School graduate, John Aubrey Davis, was determined to change that. Davis implemented several systematic boycotts, starting on U Street—something he learned at a young age from his father, John Abraham Davis, who experienced job discrimination during the Wilson era. John Aubrey Davis was also a mentee of NAACP Neval Thomas's protest. On August 28, 1933, Davis and fellow picketers marched in front of Hamburger Grill at 1211 U Street in response to the firing of three Black employees and the hiring of three white workers in replacement. The protest demonstrated the power of Black consumers, as the fired employees were rehired at the grill. The triumph sparked the formation of the New Negro Alliance (NNA), and the "Don't Buy Where You Can't Work" campaign was born. By 1938, the group claimed to have secured more than five thousand substantial jobs for Black people. The most famous of the NNA's victories was a Supreme Court win against the racist Sanitary Grocery Company near Eleventh and U. The store is now known as Safeway.[284] *Library of Congress, Prints and Photographs Division.*

ENTERTAINMENT

I went to all of the theaters. The Lincoln, the Republic, the Booker T. We even went to the Dunbar Theater, which was [at] Seventh and T Streets Northwest. These were all movie theaters that you could go to. In my parents' time, U Street was the place that you went to for the Club Valley's, and you know, the nightclubs and the good times.[285]

—Gretchen Wharton, D.C. native and
lifelong Shaw community resident and activist

Newspaper clipping from the *Afro-American* newspaper on February 27, 1951. The Howard Theatre at Seventh and T Streets opened in 1910 with 1,200 seats, hosting the most famous African American entertainers of Black Broadway, before Harlem's Apollo Theatre opened its doors in 1934. As the *Washington Bee* wrote in 1910, the Howard was "first class in every appointment, a theater for the people." The theater booked road shows, circuses, musicals and vaudeville acts. In 1934, the lines to see the Mills brothers were so large that the police had to make T Street one-way. Pearl Bailey got her show business break on the high-stepping Howardettes chorus line, and the famous trumpeter and bandleader Miles Davis also played here. The Howard premiered athletes too. Joe Louis, Jackie Robinson and Sugar Ray Robinson booked shows at the Howard as comedians and song-and-dance men. It was a place, like many others along U Street, where whites ventured into town to see Black performers. White artists and bands played at the theater, as well, and white people often made up nearly a quarter of the audience.[286] Afro-American *newspaper.*

The Lincoln Theatre on 1215 U Street, next to Ben's Chili Bowl photographed between 1980 and 2006. The theater opened in 1922, serving the city's African American community when segregation excluded Blacks from other venues. It included a movie house and a ballroom in the basement, known as the Lincoln Colonnade, and hosted jazz and big band performers, such as D.C. natives Duke Ellington and Pearl Bailey. Ella Fitzgerald, Billie Holiday, Nat King Cole, Cab Calloway, Ruth Brown, Louis Armstrong and Sarah Vaughn also graced the Lincoln stage. President Franklin Delano Roosevelt had his birthday parties at the Lincoln Colonnade. The theater closed after the 1968 race riots. It was restored and reopened in 1994.[287] Out of Black Broadway's major movie palaces, like the Republic Theatre at 1333 U Street and Booker T Theatre at 1433 U Street, the Lincoln is the only one still open today.[288] *Library of Congress, Prints and Photographs Division.*

A portrait of Duke Ellington playing the piano in Washington, D.C., at what is guessed to be the Howard Theatre in June 1946. Edward Kennedy Ellington grew up in Shaw at 1212 T Street, Northwest. T Street was a residential street for the area's respectable middle class. It was a place where government clerks, physicians and businessmen lived. As a child, Ellington took piano lessons and spent his summer afternoons selling ice cream at Griffith Stadium. The young composer played his first gig with his own band, Duke's Serenaders, at True Reformers Hall after sitting in with local bands at the corridor's Poodle Dog Cafe. At the age of fourteen, he snuck into Frank Holiday's poolroom at 624 T Street, Northwest, near the Howard Theatre. Holiday's was a place where all social classes of Black U Street mixed and mingled. Surrounded by railroad porters, dining car waiters, pianists, drummers, medical interns, gamblers and pick-pocketers, Holiday's was where Ellington learned to appreciate and maintain what his parents instilled in him at a young age—the lesson that all people, no matter the paygrade, race or background, were of equal worth. As an adult, Ellington took pride in representing his race well.[289] He made major strides in the music industry and was described as the man who "made the twentieth century swing." He was an arranger and composer for more than six thousand works over the span of his jazz career, which included performing in Washington, Harlem and traveling internationally.[290] *William P. Gottlieb/Ira and Leonore S. Gershwin Fund Collection, Music Division, Library of Congress.*

A portrait of singer and trumpet player Louis Armstrong at the aquarium in New York in July 1946. Jazz was the heartbeat of U Street. National recording stars like Louis Armstrong, Fats Waller, Mary Lou Williams and saxophonist Jimmie Lunceford could be seen live at cabarets, supper clubs and jazz joints along the strip. There was Club Bengasi at 1425 U Street, Crystal Caverns on the corner of Eleventh Street, Club Bali off Fourteenth Street, the Casbah, Murray's Palace Casino, Cafe De Luxe at Seventh and S Streets, the Dreamland Cafe and Paradise Cafe around the intersection of Seventh and T and the upscale Phoenix Inn at Thirteenth and U. The music scene on U Street was like no other, and many of the big-name artists who later participated in the Harlem Renaissance found and honed their talent on Black Broadway's streets.[291] *William P. Gottlieb/Ira and Leonore S. Gershwin Fund Collection, Music Division, Library of Congress.*

Young men stretching in gym class at Armstrong Technical High School in March 1942. Jim Crow laws made U Street the first center of African American basketball, as the sport was widely segregated elsewhere. In 1906, Black teachers weary of being ruled out of competitions with local white teams, founded the Interscholastic Athletic Association. One of the leaders was M Street graduate Ed Henderson. Organized African American basketball is said to have been founded by Henderson, who decided to start his own basketball league after being kicked out of the white Central YMCA gymnasium in 1907. Henderson gathered teams from Howard University, Twelfth Street YMCA and local high schools to play ball every Saturday night at True Reformer Hall. The games were followed by dances featuring Ellington and his band. Armstrong High had one of the better teams in the league and, in 1909, was one of the teams to compete in the first intercity series among African American players, bringing together athletes from New York and Washington.[292] *Library of Congress, Prints and Photographs Division.*

SET THE COLORED MAN FREE

The nation was on the brink of entering the Cold War when U Street's frontrunners began making headway in the local fight for civil rights, about a decade before the civil rights movement began in the mid-1950s. Carter G. Woodson had already drafted the *Journal of Negro History*, which would later blossom into the February celebration of Black History Month. Mordecai Johnson was stationed at Howard University, transforming the poorly funded institution into a success magnet. Dorothy Height was launching her civil rights career in the fight for affordable housing, and Charles Hamilton Houston was making a name for himself winning local court cases—a precursor to the famed victory of *Brown vs. Board of Education*. U Street, for the moment, was a city no longer on the rise, but on top. The District's economic and racial divide had pushed Black U Streeters to fend for themselves, and the result was a burgeoning African American community tucked away in the secret city itself. Local social and professional organizations of color grew tighter and neater during the years of Black Broadway. Churches continued to be a support system for not just parishioners but also schools and businesses of color throughout U Street.[293] The Great Depression hit Washington hard, as it did in other parts of the nation, but U Street's foundation survived throughout the '30s. At the time, the corridor was one of the largest, wealthiest and best-educated Black communities in America.[294]

During mass migrations to Washington, job lay-offs, a plummeting housing market and vanquishing family savings, U Streeters banded together to support their own. And if there was something of need that residents couldn't build or create on their own, local leaders put pressure on city government to make up the difference. The District's African American population grew tremendously during the 1940s. World War II shoved a number of southerners to Washington. Pressed by racial vehemence and agricultural despair, many migrants, Black and white, sought to start over in industrial cities like New York and Chicago. Many of the Black migrants traveling from places like Virginia and the Carolinas made D.C. their new home. By 1950, African Americans amounted to 35 percent of the city's population—the highest in Washington's history.

Still, finding work in D.C. remained tough. City and federal government, particularly in defense industries, discriminated against Black applicants and job seekers by weaving around fair-hiring protocols. For instance, out of the more than 500 workers at the city jail, workhouse and National Training School for Boys, none were Black.[295] In 1941, the U.S. Employment Service reported having issues with "skilled negro workers" job placement in defense related occupations. Out of 8,000 people added to the aviation plants payroll, only 13 were Black. In machine and tool shops, 245 out of 35,000 new employees were Black, and in electrical equipment plants, just 5 Black workers were hired in a three-month period out of 1,066 applicants.[296] Motivated to take a stand against discrimination in the workforce, Black organizers developed a plan to host a massive march on Washington.[297]

TEN, TWENTY, FIFTY THOUSAND NEGROES ON THE WHITE HOUSE LAWN

A force to be reckoned with in the labor movement, the Florida native and New York socialist A. Philip Randolph took it on himself in 1941 to mobilize civil disobedience against segregation in the armed forces. Randolph credited racism as the product of economic insecurity. He disagreed with America's capitalist order and believed it didn't benefit the poor and working-class community. Randolph once explained that "one section of the population appropriates a part of the product which others have produced without giving any equivalent exchange." It was those beliefs that prompted Randolph to visit the White House repeatedly throughout the 1940s to voice his concerns regarding European colonialism and lynching.[298] The tall, gray-haired boss of the Brotherhood of Sleeping Car Porters, the first African American labor union to sign a collective bargaining agreement with a major U.S. corporation,[299] believed the federal administration would not enforce fair labor practices until it saw "ten, twenty, fifty thousand negroes on the White House lawn."

So, Randolph put together the March on Washington Committee, which included Walter White, the executive secretary of the NAACP and adviser to First Lady Eleanor Roosevelt;[300] Frank Crosswaith of the Harlem Labor Union; Henry Craft of the Harlem YMCA; Lester Granger of the National Urban League; historian Rayford Logan; civil rights activist Bayard Rustin; and pacifist A.J. Muste. Randolph and Rustin held many of their committee meetings at U Street establishments, one being the Twelfth Street YMCA.[301] The two would later team up again in Washington for the 1963 March on Washington for Jobs and Freedom, alongside Dr. Martin Luther King Jr., where King would deliver his famous "I Have a Dream" speech. Randolph set the march date for July 1, 1941, with plans to have people of color from all over the country parade down Pennsylvania Avenue, passing in front of both houses of Congress. The proposed march developed into more than a demonstration—it mushroomed into a movement. The NAACP welcomed such a movement with open arms, pledging its full support with monetary contributions and use of its staff. The Black press gave the movement editorial help, while donations came in from women's groups, schools and churches throughout the nation.[302]

This wasn't the first time Randolph put pressure on President Franklin Delano Roosevelt to enforce fairness and equality in Washington. A few years earlier, Randolph was in the mix of Howard University's activism renaissance under the school's first Black president, Mordecai Johnson. In 1935, the National Negro Congress (NCC) was founded at Howard, and the free-spoken Randolph, who would later be called the "Father of the Civil Rights Movement,"[303] led the team. The NNC was a labor-based national coalition dedicated to fighting racial discrimination in the workplace. According to writer Erik Gellman, "The NNC sought to build a mass antiracist coalition rooted in the labor movement that could attack racial hierarchy and the economic exploitation that undergirded it. Their goal was nothing less than the evisceration of Jim Crow and the elevation of black Americans to 'first-class' citizenship—fulfilling the dreams of an egalitarian, interracial democracy first glimpsed in the Reconstruction era." The group was interested in class dynamics and stood against fascism and discrimination by stirring up resistance in the working class.

Demonstrators in the street holding signs during the March on Washington, 1963. *Library of Congress.*

This strategy differed from the NAACP's approach to warding off racism, which usually centered on broadcasting the educated "talented tenth" and elite class of Blacks. The NNC wanted to highlight the country's everyday Black laborers.[304] The NNC mostly zeroed in on issues in Chicago, New York and other industrial cities, but in Washington, the group campaigned against police brutality, what some referred to as "legal lynching." The Reconstruction era saw a number of Black recruits in the D.C. police force, but by 1933, there was one white police officer or firefighter per 153 white Washingtonians and just one Black officer or firefighter for every 2,047 Black residents. The result subjected Black residents, especially the poor, to overpolicing, verbal abuse, battering, unwarranted searches and, in some cases, death by the hands of law enforcement. The NNC, with the help of its national secretary John P. Davis, petitioned President Roosevelt to fire the police chief, fund pensions for victims' families, organize a civilian review board and suspend five officers. The campaign to end police violence, which included the petition and mass protests, was successful. The D.C. police chief Ernest Brown eventually stepped down and was replaced with a chief more open to serving the Black community.[305]

This time, Randolph's efforts triggered the drafting of legislation in favor of fair employment practices. A massive African American march on the

Lincoln Memorial would be an international embarrassment, especially while America was off fighting World War II in defense of democracy. How contradictory would America's stance in an international war be when its own citizens were still in bondage on the United States' very homefront? The threat of public outcry sent white leaders into a publicity frenzy. New York mayor Fiorello La Guardia called the March on Washington committee into conference in hopes of finding some resolve, but Randolph didn't budge. First Lady Eleanor Roosevelt, a beloved supporter of the Black community, expressed her concerns about the proposed march. She feared the demonstration could turn violent. "You know where I stand, but the attitude of the Washington police, most of them southerners, and the general feeling in Washington itself are such that I fear there may be trouble if the march occurs," Eleanor said. Still Randolph would not back down.

President Roosevelt himself eventually sent for Randolph and Walter White to meet in Washington. After meeting with various federal officials and getting no substantial results, Roosevelt inquired about exactly what Randolph wanted. Randolph responded with a demand for an executive order that quickly abolished discrimination in war industries and the armed services. So, Executive Order 8802 was drafted and issued on June 25, 1941, just a week before the march. The order would later be known as the Fair Employment Act. Officially, discrimination in defense industries based on race, creed, color or national origin was barred, and the Fair Employment Practices Committee was established to monitor defense contractors.[306] Randolph called off the march, as his proposed protest brought about the most significant federal civil rights victory since Reconstruction.[307]

U Street's elites, just like Randolph, were cooking up strategies to fight racism and empower the Black community. From faculty meetings in Howard University classrooms to having small talk over good meals at Harrison's Cafe at 455 Florida Avenue, Northwest, history makers spent their everyday lives along U Street. It was among the neighborhood lunch counters, churches, jazz clubs and libraries that U Street civil rights activists like Charles Hamilton Houston jumped in the fight for equality.[308]

CHARLES HAMILTON HOUSTON

Before Houston set the stage to kill Jim Crow, he was excelling at M Street High School near U Street. As a child, Houston was cultivated by

Washington's talented tenth community, immersed in a higher-education lifestyle of what W.E.B. DuBois described as "exceptional men."[309] As the son of Howard University–trained lawyer William Houston and Wilberforce College graduate and popular hair stylist Mary Hamilton,[310] the future Harvard Law School graduate was truly a product of his environment.

A young Houston graduated from M Street High School as valedictorian of his class and continued to Amherst College at the age of sixteen, where he enrolled as the only African American student in the class of 1911.[311] After graduating from college magna cum laude as a member of the Phi Beta Kappa honor society in 1915, he returned to U Street for two years to teach English at Howard and at his alma mater, Dunbar High. Houston enlisted in the U.S. Army during World War I as one of more than 2 million Blacks, of whom 367,000 served overseas. He served as first lieutenant of a segregated infantry unit. During his two years of service in the military, he experienced something that he was sheltered from growing up around U Street's Black elite: white aversion. Harassment, blatant racism and abuse overran his military career and forever reshaped the way he viewed his American life.[312] Houston wrote about his two years of service based in Fort Meade, Maryland:

> *The hate and scorn showered on us Negro officers by our fellow Americans convinced me that there was no sense in my dying for a world ruled by them. I made up my mind that if I got through this war I would study law and use my time fighting for men who could not strike back.*[313]

The legal work Houston began after leaving the army in 1919 would help others fight back against white opposition for the next century. As one of Houston's proteges, Justice Thurgood Marshall, said in 1978, "Whatever is done ten years from now in this country for justice and decency for American citizens, you bring it to me, and I'll be able to point out what Charlie Houston said about it back in the 1930s."[314] Shortly after Houston returned to Washington, he entered Harvard Law School to pursue his dreams of becoming a lawyer alongside his father. Just like in Houston's adolescent years, he was a top scholar in his postsecondary studies. At Harvard, he was admired by future Supreme Court justice Felix Frankfurter. Houston served as an editor on the *Harvard Law Review* in 1922, making him the first African American to hold such a title.[315] He graduated from Harvard in the top 5 percent of his class, earning a bachelor of law degree. He stayed another year to earn his doctor of juridical science and then went to the University of Madrid, where he earned a doctorate in civil law.[316] In 1924, he was admitted to the District of Columbia bar and returned home to Washington to work at his father's law firm. After years of training abroad, researching race relations and encountering prejudice along the way, home is where he set in motion the landmark civil rights case *Brown v. Board of Education.*

It was almost perfect timing when Houston began working as an attorney in the neighborhood, as Howard University's new president Mordecai Johnson was looking to upgrade the college's law school. Leading up to Johnson's induction as president, the university—what some nicknamed the Dummy's Retreat—was in upheaval. The university had earned a poor reputation in the 1920s, fitting for the poor academic standards and its leadership. A lot of the departments had lost accreditation, and the university as a whole was in financial crisis. Thanks to Howard's well-put-together facilities and prime location, there remained a shred of hope for revival. Johnson's rough Tennessee upbringing and schooling at historically black Morehouse College in Atlanta, Georgia, groomed him for such a task. Authoritative by nature and an orator since youth, Johnson had the reputation among his colleagues and employees as being tough and work driven. With ambition and vision, Johnson transformed Howard from a university on the verge of disaster to the soul of black education. Johnson had a knack for recruiting the best of the best scholars when they were on the brink of breaking into their expertise. Houston was one of those first-rate recruits.[317]

When Houston joined Johnson's team of rising intellectuals in 1924, the law school was holding classes at a university-purchased house at 420 Fifth Street, Northwest. The school remained at this site until its relocation to the main campus in 1936.[318] One of the first things on Houston's law school makeover list was shutting down the night school that had educated his father in legal studies years prior. When Houston became a professor at Howard Law, the unaccredited, open-admissions school was giving the majority of its instruction at night to cater to the enrollees who worked full-time day jobs in addition to attending the university.

On the surface, this open-admissions setup seemed like a good thing. After all, Howard Law, since its opening, had turned out 75 percent of the country's African American attorneys, Houston's father being one of them. So, what needed to be fixed or, better yet, disrupted? As writer Gary M. Lavergne recalled in Judge Robert L. Carter's autobiography, "The unaccredited school produced graduates who were not able to pass the bar exam, and as a result, they remained waiters, postal workers, and porters, as if they had never attended a law school." If Houston was going to create a

"Harvard" for Blacks and groom litigators who could challenge and change America's broken legal system, he knew that he'd have to be more selective in choosing qualified students.[319] So, he opted for quality over quantity, and the entering class size shrank to a dozen or fewer students,[320] which paired with his restructured curriculum and new roster of proficient instructors. This move didn't come without criticism of elitism, but Houston thought that admitting students who were unprepared to pass the bar after graduation was unproductive for all parties involved.

So, America's first law program specializing in civil rights began. Houston became dean of the college of law in 1930, and by 1931, the law school had earned full accreditation from the whites-only American Bar Association and was granted membership in the Association of American Law Schools without qualification. It was necessary to have more Black lawyers to uproot racial inequality in America. Unlike Houston's years in the military, this war on civil rights was a battle of the minds rather than physical force, and Houston wanted more Black brains on his team.[321]

Standing six feet tall with a disciplined demeanor, Houston was known by his colleagues to be serious and resilient. To his students, he stressed the importance of having more Black attorneys in America's legal world,[322] and in January 1935, he published an entire study on the topic. That same year, NAACP president Walter White hired him as special counsel to the justice group. In his eyes, lawyers operated the "machinery of the government" and if Blacks were going to have a fair shot at winning the fight for freedom, African Americans would need more operators behind those machines. He began his study, "The Need for Negro Lawyers," by saying:

> *The social justification for the Negro lawyer as such in the United States today is the service he can render the race as an interpreter and proponent of its rights and aspiration. There are enough white lawyers to care for the ordinary legal business of the country if that were all that was involved. But experience has proved that the average white lawyer, especially in the South, cannot be relied upon to wage an uncompromising fight for equal rights for Negroes. He has too many conflicting interests, and usually himself profits as an individual by that very exploitation of the Negro which, as a lawyer, he would be called upon to attack and destroy....According to the 1930 census there were 1,230 Negro lawyers in the United States in 1930 as against 159,735 white lawyers. These census figures list a number of Negroes as lawyers who have never passed the bar or practised a single day.[323]*

Producing skilled lawyers was a top priority for the new college dean, but he wouldn't train them to just be lawyers; he also concentrated their subject matter on studies that directly applied to the economic, political and social trials of Black people.[324]

One of Houston's first legal strategists against segregation was Baltimorean Thurgood Marshall. A young, determined Marshall commuted to Washington from Baltimore six days a week to attend class at 8:00 a.m. because he couldn't afford to live in the District, and University of Maryland Law School denied Black applicants admission. At the time of Marshall's birth in 1908, Baltimore was the country's fourth-largest urban Black population. However, Old West Baltimore, the neighborhood where Marshall grew up, was very integrated.

Marshall was taught by his father, William Marshall, at a young age to not tolerate racist remarks from whites. William Marshall was a fair-skinned well-read man who waited at Baltimore country clubs, railroad dining cars and hotels until Thurgood went to college at Lincoln University. William trained Thurgood and his eldest brother, Aubrey, to respond to race-based epithets quickly and directly, and he and his wife, Norma, paid close attention to their boys' schoolwork. Thurgood credited his innate notion to succeed and his passion for competitive debating to his in-home political and current events discussions with his father: "He did it by teaching me to argue, by challenging my logic on every point, by making me prove every statement. He never told me to be a lawyer, but he turned me into one." Marshall would go on to be the law school's most remarkable student. "While in the Law School, I served as student assistant librarian for two years, was a member of the Court of Peers for one year, and Chief Justice of the Court of Peers during the last year," Marshall reminisced. Still, he wasn't the only standout on Houston's dream team.[325]

Houston's younger cousin William Hastie was recruited to the law school's faculty by Mordecai Johnson in 1931. Hastie followed in the footsteps of his elder cousin by attending Dunbar High School, Amherst College and Harvard, where he, too, graduated with a law degree and juridical studies doctorate.[326] In 1937, President Roosevelt appointed Hastie as federal judge for the Federal District Court in the Virgin Islands, making him the first African American to serve as a federal magistrate.[327]

Other social justice pioneers who were inspired by Houston during his years at Howard included James Nabrit, who taught the first formal civil rights course offered in the United States. Nabrit's students were Spottswood Robinson and Robert Carter, who both argued portions of the *Brown v. Board*

Thurgood Marshall on September 17, 1957. *Library of Congress, Prints and Photographs Division.*

of Education case.[328] A. Leon Higginbotham also was mentored by Houston. In 1995, Higginbotham received the Presidential Medal of Freedom, the nation's highest civilian honor.[329]

Marshall became the NAACP's chief legal counsel in 1936,[330] and Hastie took over Howard Law in 1939. The tenacious group of lawyers worked together between Howard's campus and the NAACP headquarters in New York, challenging the legal system that viewed people of color as second-class citizens case by case. Although Houston died at the age of fifty-four, his university fellows carried out the legal architecture that he meticulously laid out to dismantle segregation at its core.[331]

SEPARATE IS NOT EQUAL

Houston and his team weren't the only U Streeters fed up with white hostility and racial disparities running rampant throughout the city. For instance, the New Negro Alliance had been staging series of boycotts and forming picket lines in front of businesses that refused to hire African American employees since the early 1930s. The organization campaigned against discrimination in the economic sector and aimed to improve the fortunes of Blacks by purchasing from Black businesses while simultaneously halting the practice of shopping at stores and grocers who denied African Americans employment. The strategies led by John Aubrey Davis and backed by area elites, such as Carter G. Woodson and Mary McLeod Bethune, were so successful that it inspired the local NAACP chapter to borrow the NNA's approach some years later, during the civil rights movement under the presidency of Eugene Davidson.[332] In the early 1940s, Howard students began nonviolent protests of racist businesses by sitting at whites-only counters for hours at a time, silently waiting to be served or escorted to jail.

Housing was a major issue in the city, and just like every other social sector in Washington, there was a color line when it came to residences. World War II had drained the nation's capital of space and funds. In 1934, the Alley Dwelling Authority was established to inspect and alleviate the poor conditions of alley communities where poor Blacks resided, but the mass influx of migrants to the city during the war resulted in overcrowded neighborhoods, and even the prior government protections were trumped by a lack of space and white resistance to integrate housing developments. Alley housing was supposed to be banished in 1944, but as Agnes Ernst Meyer wrote in observation of the housing dilemma, "Bad as most of these slum pigsties may be, they cannot be condemned until there is some place for the Negro to go." Real estate developers were building new homes for the masses of new white war workers, while Blacks were trapped by restrictive housing covenants and limited access to mortgage loans. Since Davis and his colleagues were attacking segregation in commerce and Houston and his attorneys were ripping apart the legal framework of segregated America, someone had to take on the task of improving housing conditions. Dorothy Height was the right woman for the job.

Height moved to D.C. in 1939 at twenty-seven years old. She was born in Richmond, Virginia, and possessed a master's degree from New York University. As an activist and leader at the corridor's Phyllis Wheatley YWCA, she wanted to take more hands-on measures to ensure that people of color had more housing options. The YWCA offered affordable housing, as it still does today, to low-income women, but Height believed more needed to be done to meet the demand of war workers. She conducted her own survey on the living conditions of residents and reported the findings to federal housing officials. Eventually, Height's demands were met, and hotels were built for Black war workers, one being the 322-bed Lucy Diggs Slowe Hall

Administrative staff members at the Lucy D. Slowe Residence Hall, which cost $760,000. This was the first government constructed hotel for Negro women war workers in Washington, D.C, around 1942. *Library of Congress, Prints and Photographs Division, Farm Security Administration/Office of War Information Black-and-White Negatives.*

at 1919 Third Street, Northwest.[333] Height wasn't alone in the equal housing rights battle. Houston gained a major victory in 1948, when he argued and won the Supreme Court case *Hurd v. Hodge*, which ended the practice of restrictive covenants on housing deeds that forbid the sale of property to certain groups of people—in this case a Black couple.[334] Houston wasn't alive to see the result of his next big blow to legalized segregation, but it would forever change the country's education system.

D.C. Black public schools struggled in the '30s and '40s as demographics in the city spiraled into overpopulation of Black schools and shrinking of white schools as white families moved to the suburbs. By 1950, African American students were the majority in Washington public schools. In fact, by 1957, Washington had become the first city in the United States with African Americans as the majority population.[335] Due to a law made nearly a century earlier to help Black schools with funding, the law was now causing Black institutions to receive less funding than their white counterparts. The 1864 law had required the city to allocate school funds based on the number of white and Black students in the decennial census, and now, Blacks were no longer the District's school-age minority.

Judine Bishop, daughter of Gardener "Bish" Bishop, was affected by the education crisis. Judine attended overcrowded Browne Junior High School, and this didn't fare well with her outspoken father. "The U Street Barber," as some referred to him, had grown to hate white people due to injustices he suffered growing up in Rocky Mount, North Carolina, and didn't care much more for those he called "highfalutin blacks." When Judine was subjected to crammed classrooms and reduced instruction time at Browne, Bishop took action. Just a mile away, Eliot Junior High School had more than enough space for its white students. Bishop and other concerned parents wanted his children to be transferred to the underpopulated white high school. In 1947, a group of parents headed by Bishop formed the Consolidated Parent Group Inc. After months of protests, Bishop turned to Houston for help, and the two formulated a plan to desegregate area schoolyard playgrounds.

Due to a heart condition that would later be the cause of Houston's premature death, the acclaimed lawyer handed the case over to Nabrit, who took the case to the Supreme Court. In 1950, Bishop led eleven Black children to Anacostia's recently opened John Philip Sousa Junior High School, but the kids were refused admission. Nabrit filed a lawsuit in 1951. The case would be known as *Bolling v. Sharpe*, titled after one of the dismissed students, Spottswood Thomas Bolling Jr. The case was placed in a collection of similar cases, including the famous *Brown v. Board of Education*. On May 17, 1954, the *Brown* decision ruled racial segregation in public schools unconstitutional, abolishing school segregation in D.C. and forty-eight states. The *Bolling* case was won along with *Brown*, but its argument had gone a step further than the more popular case, which proposed that African American schools were not equal to the white schools available in Topeka. Nabrit argued that separate can never be equal when it comes to education.[336]

The ruling made integration in schools the law, but it would be several years later before all public schools abided by the court decision. It wasn't until 1960, when Ruby Bridges stepped foot into the all-white William Frantz Elementary School in Louisiana, that the first elementary school in the South was integrated.[337]

Not only was integration of public schools slow moving, but Jim Crow laws were still in effect, and African Americans were still plagued by voter restrictions. Black people throughout the country were often denied the right to vote based on unfair literacy tests and poll taxes. For Washingtonians, the government was still without self-governance.[338] District residents, Black and white, had no vote in the city's affairs and hadn't since the Board of Public Works was established in 1874 (see chapter 3).[339] Without local home rule and national enfranchisement, Black people in D.C. were at a major disadvantage. As America was propelled into the civil rights movement in 1954, voting would have to be at the top of the agenda if Jim Crow was going to be expelled before the turn of the century.

Mordecai Johnson stressed the importance of fair voting practices at Bethel AME in Baltimore on January 10, 1954:

> *The leaders of the Republican and Democratic parties have got to decide whether they are going to override segregation and set the colored man free. We colored people should be as politically active in the next five years as we can conceive it to be possible. We must ask every candidate for governor, every candidate for senator, and every candidate for public office in the state or nation these specific questions. If the answer is "no," we must prayerfully and lovingly vote these candidates down. If the answer is "yes," we must support them and them alone is all salvation. We cannot leave them alone to decide the salvation of our country.*[340]

CIVIL RIGHTS ACT

Washington was a well-suited place to spotlight the civil rights movement in the 1960s. Several young radicals had set up shop on or near U Street and were vocal about wanting home rule and equitable community resources, taking note from sit-ins and freedom rides that were already underway in the South. So, in 1963, the march that was promised some twenty years earlier came to fruition at the Lincoln Memorial in a famed rally for African American fairness and freedom.

The March on Washington for Jobs and Freedom attracted a crowd of more than 350,000 participants. Local and national groups such as pacifist organization Congress of Racial Equality (CORE), the Student Non-Violent Coordinating Committee (SNCC), the National Urban League and Martin Luther King Jr.'s Southern Christian Leadership Conference (SCLC) banded together to lobby for voting rights.[341] The local SCLC was headed by Dunbar High School graduate Walter Fauntroy, who helped organize the successful march with the help of fellow Washington

Coordinating Committee members Julius Hobson, Sterling Tucker and D.C. NAACP's Edward A. Hailes. The Civil Rights Act of 1964, which banned discrimination in public places and enforced the right to vote, was passed into law in response to the 1963 demonstration in Washington. A year later, the Voting Rights Act of 1965 was passed to provide additional protections for African Americans at the ballots in response to the gruesome nationally televised March on Selma. The victories of the civil rights movement were major but short-lived.

Two weeks after President Johnson signed the Civil Rights Act of 1964, a six-day riot in Harlem erupted after an off-duty cop shot and killed a fifteen-year-old black student. Riots in the cities of Philadelphia, Rochester, New York, Newark, New Jersey and Detroit followed. By 1968, a buildup of racial frustration from lack of government power, over policing and decades of overt discrimination had reached the doors of the corridor. In a matter of two days, the neighborhoods along Seventh Street and up Fourteenth, which the first-freed, talented tenth and civil rights heroes had worked hard to birth and protect, were burning in flames.[342]

8

IF WE OWN THE STORY,
WE OWN THE PLACE

UStreet knows how to survive. Black U Streeters, especially, have
withstood the test of time. Whether it was slavery, Black Codes,
disenfranchisement, the Great Depression, Jim Crow, race riots,
a crack cocaine epidemic or metro construction, the heart of Black
Washington[343] never stopped beating. Even now in the twenty-first century,
behind a heavy fog of gentrification, there remains spirit, energy, rhythm,
unity and hope.

It's this hope that established the self-help organization PRIDE
Incorporated near the intersections of Sixteenth and U during the Black
Power movement.[344] It's the same local pride that inspired '70s funk band
Parliament-Funkadelic to label D.C. "Chocolate City," a title that would
be fitting for the neighborhood of U Street throughout the '70s and '80s.[345]
It's the same energy that gave the Cardozo High School band an upbeat to
step to when the Shaw Metro subway stations opened in 1991.[346] And it's
the same spirit that filled the counters of Ben's Chili Bowl on the night of
November 4, 2008, when America's first African American president was
declared.[347] And in 2019, it's the same rhythm that gave hundreds of Black
U Streeters a voice to rally "Don't Mute D.C." on the corner of Seventh
Street and Florida Avenue, Northwest, in a successful effort to keep the city's
home-grown go-go music alive.[348]

In recalling how the area has transformed over the ages, there's no doubt
that present-day U Street is far from how Martin Luther King Jr. described
Shaw in 1967, as "one of Washington's most neglected areas."[349] U Street,

like many other neighborhoods in D.C., has undergone serious polishing in recent years, and the multimillion-dollar condos, quaint cappuccino bars, upscale culinary kitchens, yoga studios and clean streets attracted an influx of new neighbors. The majority of the new neighbors moving into District areas such as Logan Circle, Petworth, Columbia Heights and Shaw, are not Black. In fact, according to a 2019 study by the Institute on Metropolitan Opportunity, Washington has experienced the most dramatic gentrification and displacement of any American city from 2002 to 2016. The study explains that District neighborhoods "have seen overall population growth of 19 percent, and white population growth of a staggering 202 percent." In particular, Shaw's low-income population has dropped 57 percent, according to the same study.[350] So, some believe that the future of U Street's African American history and culture is in jeopardy, and there remains the mystery of how the dream and fight for a better community became the reality of residents who have little to no roots in the corridor's colorful past. Darren Jones, Ward 1 native, and president of the Pleasant Plains Civic Association since 1996, believes that U Street will never go back to the way it was:

> *A lot of the history that was there, a lot of that jazz. A lot of the home-grown music that we used to be able to go down to U Street and enjoy, a lot of that has disappeared now.*
>
> *You have people with higher incomes moving in and enjoying the name of U Street and the people who kind of built the reputation. We can walk through there now, and we can enjoy Ben's Chili Bowl or stop into other shops, but we won't ever be able to live down there anymore.*[351]

The urban displacement that Jones describes is a challenge for not just D.C. but also for metropolitan areas throughout America. The process of gentrification—real estate investments that raise the prices of homes in a low-income neighborhood, accompanied by an influx of middle-class or affluent people moving into the area, usually resulting in poorer residents moving out of the area—is one that has affected the neighborhoods of Los Angeles, San Diego,[352] New York City, Baltimore, Chicago and Philadelphia, among others, over the last two decades. Gentrification is an age-old concept, dating to the '60s in some places.[353]

So, when did the demographic shift begin on U Street? Some say the abolishment of Jim Crow paired with desegregation and integration motivated Black Washingtonians to emigrate out of the corridor. Others pinpoint the decline of U Street's African American population to high crime rates and slumlords during the '70s and '80s. Others believe the revitalization of the neighborhood by way of the Metrorail construction and the opening of the Frank D. Reeves Municipal Center stimulated gentrification. Research on the neighborhood proves that all of these factors have played parts in U Street's gradual yet radical cultural turning point. Community narratives throughout this chapter give personal accounts of these significant events and provide inside perspectives on how U Street unfolded into the multicultural economic attraction of today.

PEPPER SPRAY IN THE AIR

Darren Jones grew up on Hobart Place in Northwest, D.C., and was serving on the city's Advisory Neighborhood Commission (ANC) for Ward 1B, which services South Columbia Heights, Shaw and LeDroit Park, when the Metro was being developed on U Street. The ANC was a product of the 1973 Home Rule Act, where Washingtonians, after a century of waiting for self-governance, were granted the right to elect and appoint a mayor and council to oversee the city.[354] The historic vote elected Washington's first home rule and African American mayor, Walter Edward Washington, in 1974. D.C. has elected only Black mayors ever since.[355] The ANC began operating in 1976 "to bring government closer to the people, and to bring the people closer to government." Commissioners represent every two thousand residents, serving two-year terms. They are the voices for the wards when it comes to city service recommendations and complaints in regard to sanitation, safety and budget.[356]

At the age of twenty-three, Jones was elected as a commissioner, and his neighborhoods covered lower Georgia Avenue down to the U Street corridor. At the time, he worked with railway constructors to do "right" by the people on U Street because developers had opened trenches along the row. This was bad for business. Customers could hardly travel through the roads to patronize their favorite stores, salons, pharmacies and banks. Eventually, a lot of businesses, Black-owned among others, left the area, unable to survive otherwise. This struck another blow to the well-known Black commercial and residential hub that had already been hard hit by drugs, crime and, of course, the 1968 riots.

Jones vividly recalled the April riots and the military men riding through Fourteenth Street in jeeps holding guns. He said the assassination of Martin

Lee's Flower and Card Shop during the construction of the metro in 1990. *Lee's Flower and Card Shop.*

Luther King Jr., along with the reactive rampage, brought a somber mood to U Street:

> *I remember in '68 when Dr. King died. I remember that evening how all of the parents just all seemed to be so angry. And everybody seemed to be angry. And I remember at Monroe Elementary School, when I went to school, the teachers were crying, and I don't think I've ever experienced that before or after. The teachers cried, and they showed us a short film of Dr. King. I mean, as students, we were young. It didn't hit us like that, but the teachers cried, and I mean, they were very committed to us, and they were very committed to the neighborhood.*
>
> *And then we had the riots on Seventh Street and Fourteenth Street. And there was the stuff that they were spraying. The pepper spray in the air, so when you came outside, my mother would give us a wet rag to put over our noses because it was so strong, even though we were blocks away, we could smell all of the pepper spray in the air....We called it tear gas at the time.*[357]

Urban ghettos were enraged around the country in the mid-1960s, weighed down by poor living conditions and white hostility. As Attorney General Robert F. Kennedy warned in the winter of 1962, "a major explosion in the District of Columbia" would be underway if the way of life for impoverished residents didn't improve.[358] That explosion took place after the most visible spokesperson for the civil rights movement, Dr. Martin Luther King Jr., was assassinated on the balcony of the Lorraine Motel in Memphis, Tennessee, on April 4, 1968, at 7:05 p.m. An hour after he was shot, King was dead. The following hour, President Lyndon B. Johnson gave a national address mourning the loss of this "outstanding leader" and pleading with citizens to follow the nonviolent example of King in reaction to his tragic murder. By 9:25 p.m., vandalism and looting on Fourteenth Street had begun.

Clusters of African American frontrunner groups were stationed at or near Fourteenth and U Streets, which made the neighborhood a continued center for activism, but in this case, it would be the center of unorganized rage. The headquarters of SNCC and the local offices of the Southern Christian Leadership Conference and the NAACP were in the immediate area. Initially, a peaceful group of residents were led by former SNCC national chairman Stokley Carmichael up Fourteenth Street and the U Street corridor to ask store managers to shut down their businesses in honor

D.C. riot scenes in the area of Fourteenth and Seventh Streets, Northwest, on April 8, 1968. *Library of Congress, Prints and Photographs Division.*

of King. The businesses complied, but once the crowds of protesters swelled and the window of the prejudiced Peoples Drug Store was smashed and the glass of the white-owned Republic Theatre was broken, Carmichael realized that the situation had gotten out of control.[359]

By the end of the night, 200 stores had been damaged, 150 stores had been looted, seven fires had been set, two hundred people were arrested—fifty of whom were juveniles—thirty people were injured and there was one fatality. The arson, shouting, beating, break-ins and demonstrations against the metropolitan police force continued over the weekend. White and Jewish businesses were targeted in the looting attacks—a response to grievances of unfair pricing and racial profiling that had plagued Blacks in their own community for years. Some Black businesses were spared by writing "soul brother" on their storefronts. The protests expanded past Fourteenth and Seventh Streets and overflowed into Northeast's H Street. Things quieted down after thirteen thousand army soldiers and National Guard troops were called in to take control of the city, but the area of U Street was left in rubble.[360]

A SHELL OF ITS ORIGINAL YEARS

Ernie Jarvis, the maternal grandson of blood plasma pioneer Dr. Charles Drew and paternal great-grandson of William Ernest Jarvis, founder of U Street's famed Jarvis Funeral Home at 1432 U Street, has deep connections to the corridor. His mother, Charlene Drew Jarvis, is a six-time elected D.C. councilmember, and his father, W. Ernest Jarvis, along with running the family funeral home, co-owned a nightclub on Ninth and Florida Avenue called the Hollywood in the '70s.

The late '60s and '70s were a trying time for U Streeters. Jarvis, a teenager during these years, can remember Black people having little money and living in a corridor overrun by heroin:

Post the '68 riots, there was some decline in the neighborhood. Our community was really affected by the riots, [it] certainly burned out businesses, people displaced out of housing, out of businesses, and during that decline, at the same time, we had troops returning home from the Vietnam War, and they unfortunately were not integrated back into American society.... There were many troops who served valiantly but developed drug addictions, and they came back to that particular area....There were open drug air markets during that time in the '70s.

A lot of the businesses were shut down. There were a number of car dealers on Fourteenth Street, there were places where you could buy retail items, you could buy washers and dryers it was really a self-sustaining community, and a lot of that of the glory years dissipated during those tough times.[361]

Jarvis described U Street as a shell of its original years, when it was graced by the likes of top entertainers like Cab Calloway. The boarded-up buildings, vacant lots and barricaded stores lining Fourteenth Street and Seventh Street showed that the corridor was in desperate need of refurbishing. The dirt-cheap housing prices would eventually lure young white professionals, money-hungry developers and house flippers to the area at the start of gentrification, but in the early to mid-1970s, white families and some well-off Black families were moving out of the area and into the suburbs. The crime wave was also subsiding, and the city was in the process of reestablishing itself as the capital of Black America. An influx of Latino migration to D.C. was happening around this time, too, but according to the 1970 census, African Americans were a substantial majority of D.C.'s population, totaling 70 percent of all residents.[362]

Chocolate City was on the rise, and it was nothing short of a good time, especially along the corridor, where at the height of the Black Power movement, one could listen to poet Gaston Neal at his institution on Fourteenth street, the New School for Afro-American Thought. The corridor was where partiers frequented Chez Maurice on Ninth and Florida Avenue. It's where residents hand danced and strutted in Chuck Taylors and blew out their hair locks.[363] Along the corridor, folks could hitch a ride to a Redskins football game with the neighborhood's proclaimed "Mayor of Ninth Street," Jim Shay, and into the '80s, they could bounce to the Chuck Brown–created go-go beat at the Howard Theatre near Sixth and T Streets, Northwest, on Friday nights.[364]

Jarvis remembered hanging out on the town with his father during U Street's showy years:

They [father and grandfather] *lived in the street. On U Street, they had the ability and personality to engage with everyone because in the funeral business you engage with everyone....They were night owls, and I went with my father to every bar, every speakeasy, every club up and down U Street and Ninth Street. I probably met during that period of time*

every numbers guy. There were people with nicknames as of White Top
Simkins, who was a numbers guy. It was just really one community you
knew everyone from the doctors and lawyers to the ladies of the evening.

I went with my father to places where you had to be searched for guns,
but I never felt uncomfortable because we were the undertakers. Nobody
really wanted to mess with the undertakers.

The funeral home that began in the 1920s closed its doors in 1985, but its legacy lives on. Jarvis believes his forefathers would "roll over" if they saw how U Street has been swallowed by gentrification today.[365]

100,000 NEW RESIDENTS

When D.C. mayor Anthony Williams began his second term in 2003, he promised 100,000 new residents in the area. Williams has more than exceeded that promise.[366] As of 2019, Washington is home to 705,749 people. African Americans are no longer the majority of the population. Both Blacks and whites are the majority races in D.C., with each race holding 46 percent of the city's population.[367] This is a major contrast from the 1970 census and continues to be a noticeable variation, as not only have more non-Black residents moved into the District, but businesses, lounges, housing complexes, bookstores and brunch eateries have also settled in to cater to the new wave of neighbors.

For many years, residents of color on U Street went without immediate access to large grocery stores and had to rely on convenience stores, carryouts and small markets for refreshments. As one resident put it, "There was nothing in reach" until integration.[368] Carryouts like AM.PM faithfully offered soul food takeout to working African Americans until its doors shuttered in 2010, due to "lease issues." Since 2014, Provision No. 14 has occupied the carryout's former space with a menu appealing to the new class of high-income, majority white U Streeters. Provision's American fare menu is complemented by other upscale restaurants scaling Fourteenth Street, which cater to the multicultural young entrepreneurs of the area,[369] including Le Diplomate and its popular outdoor patio and Pearl Dive Oyster Palace, which serves "the widest variety of high quality oysters." The corridor is once again a vibrant place of choice and variety, but only for those who can afford to choose.

Nonprofit social services like Fourteenth Street's Martha's Table, Central Union Mission at Fourteenth and R Streets, Northwest, and the Elizabeth Taylor Medical Center have all moved out of the area after aiding the corridor's less fortunate for the last three or four decades. Central Union Mission, like several other U Street landmarks, has been replaced with luxury apartment buildings named after the enterprises or artists who created the history of U Street. There's the Langston Lofts on Thirteenth and V, Mission at Fourteenth and R and the Ellington at Thirteenth and U Streets.

So, what pushed U Street to become the home of organic food markets and apartments that rent two-bedrooms for $7,000 a month?[370] Former mayor Williams credits the catalyst of U Street's economic renaissance to his predecessors' development of the Frank D. Reeves Municipal Center:

> *I mean, demographically, it's become a much more diverse population. It was certainly predominately African American. In terms of the building situation, you had many, many vacant lots all the way up from U Street all the way up to Columbia Heights, Mount Pleasant. I mean, there were just blocks of rubble left over from the riots. On U Street, you had a lot of abandoned buildings. A lot of vacant storefronts. But you did have Marion Barry put in the Reeves Center on the corner of Fourteenth and U, which I think was a part of a catalyst, certainly. The city had refurbished the Lincoln Theatre, which I think was a positive development on U Street, and all of this happened before I got there.*
>
> *You know, the difference between then and now is you have a much more robust economy in terms of taxes paid by the residents who live there now. By the businesses who were there in terms of sales tax. So, it's a much more prosperous area than it was prior.*

Before being elected as mayor in 1998, Williams was the independent chief financial officer of D.C. His job was created in 1994, after Congress established a control board over Washington because, as Williams explained, "The city had run out of cash," and he was given the responsibility of keeping D.C.'s finances and budget in order.[371] The city had made ground-breaking accomplishments during the Marion Barry era. Barry, raised and educated in Tennessee, moved to D.C. in 1965 to reboot the Washington chapter of SNCC. During this time, Barry initiated the Free D.C. Movement, drawing admiration from the area's poor Blacks as he dared the city's residents to boycott businesses that were not in favor of home rule.[372]

Mayor Marion Barry speaks at the opening of the Shops at National Place at Thirteenth and F Streets in the 1980s. *Library of Congress, Prints and Photographs Division.*

In 1970, a non-voting delegate was added to the House of Representatives to represent D.C. Walter Fauntroy took office in 1971 as the first to hold the position. Fauntroy, pastor of New Bethel Baptist Church, believed community activism was his religious duty. During his leadership, he secured $92 million in federal funding to fix up the commercial corridors of Fourteenth, U and Seventh Streets through his Model Inner-City Community Organization, although he ran into opposition with competing organizations. Fauntroy also convinced Metro line planners to include African American neighborhoods in the routes during the early planning years. In 1976, the subway began operating. The transit was completed in 1991.

Barry won the mayoral race at the end of the '70s, and by then, the distribution of federal funding was in the hands of President Jimmy Carter and then President Ronald Reagan, who were not as generous as Nixon and Johnson. Reckless spending of Barry's district government had also left regional officials short-funded. So, Barry strategically chose the site of a municipal office building to be built at Fourteenth and U, where it still stands today. The Frank D. Reeves Municipal Center opened in 1986 and welcomed a healthy flow of middle-class civil servants for the first time in years. The center was the economic turnaround for U Street, and one

Washington Post columnist, Courtland Milroy, wrote, that a "white tornado" was sweeping the neighborhood "clean of litter and junkies." Unfortunately, crack cocaine arrived in Washington that same year, and crime rates skyrocketed. Notorious kingpin Rayful Edmond III and his gang wreaked havoc on the city, spending time at Florida Avenue Grill on Eleventh street and selling to users from Florida to New York Avenue. The school system declined, and affordable housing projects hosted open drug markets. From 1984 to 1989, there was a 43 percent increase in arrested adults testing positive for cocaine.[373]

I JUST DON'T WANT TO PUSH NOBODY OUT

Wanda Henderson was working at African American beauty salon Natural Motions off Georgia Avenue in Northwest during the crack epidemic. She recalled, "It destroyed a lot of families. A lot of children went through without a parent because they were on drugs. There were crack babies being born. It was just trying, murders in the city. It was just too many things going on in the black community."

The Ledroit Park native and member of St. Martin's church said that during Shaw's drug years she worked fifteen-hour days to stay busy and keep away from the drug abuse areas. Her hard work paid off, and after eighteen years of working on Georgia Avenue, she had earned enough money to open her own 1,500-square-foot shop at Twelfth and U, paying one dollar per square foot for rent in 1997. She said she was successful on U Street and had noticed the area was changing. "Gentrification was just about starting; the area had changed, new buildings had started coming up…and the area was drug free….It was more foot traffic, car traffic, more restaurants, more clubs opening, so U Street became the hot spot."

Henderson moved her salon to Seventh Street in 2003 and was paying $2,000 a month in rent until developers took over the building and raised her monthly expenses to about $3,800 in 2004. Henderson left the space at 1851 Seventh Street, Northwest, to style hair in another place while she worked out a leasing agreement with the developers—a battle that she said was very tough and at times felt like harassment. Henderson was able to move back to her Seventh Street salon in 2014, something she is very proud of, but as of this writing, she is paying $6,560.05 a month in rent, plus an additional approximate $24,000 a year in property taxes and utilities.

Stories like Henderson's are not uncommon along the corridor, as more and more residents are constantly out priced in the neighborhoods where they went to grade school, made lifetime friends, buried loved ones and earned a living. As she said in reference to the rapid displacement, "I welcome the people in, I just don't want to push nobody out." Henderson was fortunate to be able to keep her beauty parlor open, but most longtime Black-owned enterprises cannot. Henderson, like several other native residents, is hoping for legislation that will better protect the history of U Street by regulating the real estate market and providing more support for Black commerce.[374]

In October 2019, historical U Street protests resulted in legislation being passed to declare go-go music the official genre of D.C. It was a historical win for both the city and the neighborhood of U Street.

In April 2019, Shaw luxury apartment residents pushed to shut off the go-go music playing outside a Metro PCS storefront at Florida Avenue and Seventh Street, Northwest. The complaint put U Street, for the first time in decades, back at the center of the fight for equality. Community activists, go-go bands and thousands of Washingtonians of all races took to the U Street corridor to defend the playing of the music that had been part of the area's Black culture for about twenty years. For months, live music was performed on the block in nonviolent protest as people posted #DontMuteDC to their social media pages. It didn't take long for the movement to become national news, and suddenly, in a neighborhood that some would say had misplaced its history, roots and soul, there was a resurgence of the heartbeat of Black Washington.[375] The sound of the beat was different from the era of Black Broadway's smooth jazz, and it was louder than the bop from the Chocolate City era. This was a sound that had progressed past bondage, through segregation and had outlived integration. It was the mix of backgrounds, genders, skin tones, education and pay grades mashed into one groovy Congo beat. It was the sound of justice, of memory—a sweet reminder that the voices of U Street will never die out.

So, whether the notables of U Street have migrated out of the corridor or are still serving hot chili half smokes on Ben's Ali Way, as long as there's a story to tell then, like former D.C. councilmember and Civil War Museum director Dr. Frank Smith told U Street researcher Stephanie Barbara Frank, "if we own the story, we own the place."[376]

U STREET AND THE BLACK MECCA: BE NOT FORGOTTEN, BE NOT DENIED

Each generational change in a community laments the loss of the past and a fear of the future. "Remember the good ole days" is the refrain. And then someone will add, "Well, the good ole days were not always so good." Indeed, these word ring loud and clear about Black Broadway, the U Street corridor, the Shaw-Cardozo-LeDroit Park neighborhood, also known as the Black Mecca of America.

There is no denying that the U Street corridor emerged between the late nineteenth century and the 1970s as one of the most illustrious communities of Black excellence, progress and envy in America. Author Briana Thomas makes the case convincingly, graphically, empirically and with style. Black intellectuals, politicians, businessmen and women, artists and everyday travelers would purposely stop in Washington, D.C., to visit the U Street corridor and bask in the sunshine of Black excellence. A walk down U Street on a Sunday afternoon was not just a walk; it was a promenade. "Men had to wear ties and women wore white gloves," so went the motto. U Street was Black America's Champs D'Elyse. After church on Sundays, it was the place to see and be seen. Famed photographer Addison Scurlock captured it frequently. If you were photographed by Scurlock, you had made it in the annals of the best and the brightest of Black America frolicking U Street.

Black people throughout America made it a point to visit the Black Mecca and its gleaming crown jewel Howard University. Intellectuals, politicians, artists, lawyers, doctors and men and women of letters referred to poet Georgia Douglas Johnson's home as the Halfway House because it was halfway between Black Atlanta's famed Morehouse and Spelman and Harlem, New York. Johnson's house at 1461 S Street, just steps from U Street, was the go-to venue for monthly literary salons that featured Black intelligentsia like Langston Hughes, Zora Neale Hurston, Alain Locke, Dr. Charles Drew, Oscar DePriest, Ernest Everett Just, Jessie Redmon Fauset, Angelina Grimké, Aaron Douglas, Mary Church Terrell, Carter G. Woodson, Charles Hamilton Houston, Anna Julia Cooper, Lois Mailou Jones, Alma Thomas, Madame Evanti, Thurgood Marshall and W.E.B. Du Bois. Yes, those were the glory days.

But those glory days were not always so glorious. It would be easy to romanticize the U Street corridor as the Black Mecca where everything was enviable within the most successful Black community in America, where Blacks were known as the Black bourgeoisie along U Street and LeDroit Park and, a few blocks west, as the Black aristocracy in the Strivers Section of Dupont Circle. In this community adjacent to U Street lived Mary Church Terrell, Langston Hughes, Charles Hamilton Houston, the Murray Family (Black printing business), General Benjamin Davis, Charles and Louis Douglass. It was also the headquarters of Delta Sigma Theta and Kappa Alpha Psi. These were heady days and spaces in the Black Mecca.

But Jim Crow, segregation and violence against Black people was frequent and debilitating in these neighborhoods during the years of the *Black Mecca*. Let us not be too romantic. Jim Crow, also known as domestic terrorism, was real. Blacks could not go to the National Zoo on Easter Sunday, as was the tradition in our nation's Capital for White people. Blacks could not try on clothes or a hat in downtown clothing stores. Black children hungry for a sandwich could not sit at lunch counters in downtown department stores. Blacks could not attend "whites-only" theaters. Blacks could not sit in a park on Sunday afternoon in a white community because "No Blacks, Jews and Dogs Allowed" signs prohibited their entry. The city had a 90 percent white police force when the city was 75 percent Black. What's wrong with this picture? Black people were not registered to vote and could not serve on juries. Blacks could not elect their own local or national representatives. The five universities in the city were reserved for whites only. White supremacy ruled.

No, the good ole days were not so good. But the heroic struggles of Black youth and white allies in the South ushered in a new era: the modern civil rights movement. Sparked by the horrific torture and killing of Emmett Till in 1955, an uprising of militant youth and church-based moral movements led to the passage of the 1964, 1965 and 1968 Civil Rights Acts, which opened doors, housing, libraries, schools and jobs to Black people hitherto denied. And with the loosening of Jim Crow segregation, Black people who could move, moved. Middle- and professional-class Blacks left their old segregated neighborhoods for greener grass and newer communities. Just as generations of Italians, Polish, Irish and Jewish people left their old communities when they had an opportunity, Blacks did as well. That's a basic American ideal: the next generation moves out and on up. Hello, *The Jeffersons*.

Blacks moved to the suburbs in the 1950s–'80s because they could. Prince George's County, Maryland, became a new Black Mecca in the 'burbs. And just as this movement began, a hot bullet sliced through the cool Memphis air, entering Dr. King's body and felling this man of nonviolence and peace. Pent up rage at three hundred–plus years of white supremacy exploded onto 130 cities rising up and rebelling against his murder. From April 4 through 11, smoke, fire, looting, arson and death rained down on cities and mini Black meccas everywhere. When the rebellion ended in mid-April 1968, American cities looked like war zones. Indeed, they were. A war against white supremacy, police brutality, segregation, insult and three hundred years of denial wrecked and weakened segregated Black American enclaves.

With businesses and homes destroyed, people's spirits were destroyed as well. Once proud sections of Black businesses lay in ruins. Almost immediately, an exodus occurred. D.C.'s U Street corridor was devastated. Black communities now entered a long period of isolation and shock. Boarded up Black homes, businesses and institutions gave rise to communities that attracted crime, drugs and violence. As community deteriorated in these Black enclaves, the exodus increased. The 75 percent Black population decreased to 65 percent in 1980, 60 percent in 1990, 50 percent in 2000 and 45 percent in 2020, leaving behind vacant homes, businesses, churches, social venues and institutions. For thirty years, from 1968 until 1998, Black flight out of Shaw, Cardozo and LeDroit Park left gaping holes in the community, which were filled first by an immigrant Ethiopian community fleeing their own civil wars in Africa. When Mayor Marion Barry opened the Reeves Center at Fourteenth and U Streets in 1986, the Metro opened at Thirteenth and U Street in 1991 and then Dr. Frank Smith opened the African American Civil War Memorial and Museum at Tenth and U Street in 1998, the community began to bounce back. The 1992 dot-com explosion brought a renewed sense and lifeblood to urban communities, and real estate values began to bounce back. Young people tiring of commutes from suburbs began to flock to cheap real estate opportunities in urban centers, with Shaw, Cardozo, LeDroit Park and Columbia Heights leading the way. Soon cafés, cinemas, coffee shops, boutiques, dog parks and bike lanes began to pop up as fast as beer gardens. Generational change was happening again. By 2005, gentrification was on.

By 2019, the U Street corridor had become the most gentrified community in the Unites States. Home values skyrocketed. Businesses boomed. Restaurants and beer gardens exploded on the scene. Single-family homes became multimillion-dollar condos. Large luxury apartments grew up on spaces that were once burned out by the 1968 rebellion. Those Blacks who moved out did so because they could. They left because poor schools and dangerous communities pushed them out. In came a new generation. The city's population went from 570,000 in 1980 to more than 705,000 in 2019, with 1,000 people per month moving into one of the "hippest cities in nation." U Street today bustles as it did back in the Black Broadway days, only rather than it being mostly Black, it is now one of the most diverse communities in America.

And who can complain that U Street now reflects Dr. Martin Luther King Jr.'s vision of a community where all of God's children can eat, drink, laugh, live, play and walk together down the street in harmony and friendship. This is U Street today—Dr. King's vision actualized.

But there is a *but*. U Street is back. And its *Black Broadway* vibe still exists at numerous theaters and clubs, such as the Lincoln, the Howard, 930 Club and Ben's Next Door. Even Bohemian Caverns is coming back. The street is packed in the evening, with new restaurants, pop-up music and street performers. Over twenty-five murals adorn the street, remembering and celebrating D.C.'s Black history and culture. But at the same time, Black institutions, businesses and social clubs that were the essence of Black excellence on the corridor are rapidly disappearing. Some of the historic churches that were open since the Civil War are closing due to a lack of attendance as the Black population declines, leaving the city for greener pastures. Where there was once over two hundred Black businesses lining U Street from 1910 to 1970, only five of them are still operating today: the Howard Theatre, Prince Hall Masonic Temple, Lee's Flower and Card Shop, Industrial Bank and Ben's Chili Bowl. Currently, there are only fifteen Black American businesses on U Street. This trend sees no end in sight. Washington, D.C., is a destination city for young, aggressive entrepreneurs, professionals and urban pioneers who find diversity, culture and history attractive themes when looking for a place to live, work, learn and play.

The challenge for local residents who cherish their history and culture is to stay vigilant and not be erased out of existence. Black businesses must band together to help other Black businesses stay, succeed and start new ones. City elected officials must find ways to give tax breaks and incentives not just to new developers coming into the corridor but also to those longtime historic Black businesses that hung on to U Street during the dark and dangerous years. Property tax increases, although good for the local economy, should not run longtime minority- and women-owned businesses out of the city.

Local residents must be conscious of where they shop and from whom they buy. Black residents, indeed, all local residents must renew their efforts to shop Black and support Black businesses. Howard University is still the incubator for Black excellence in the U Street corridor and must redouble its efforts to preserve and protect its history and culture in this community. Howard continues to pump new blood into the body politic of the Black Mecca. Go-go music, the sound of D.C., cannot allow newcomers to stop its sound and beat from "busting loose." *Black Mecca* aficionados must stand fast to their history and culture with more street art, performances and renewed Black entrepreneurship. Let a thousand murals bloom. Let a million go-go beats go on. D.C. used to boast five Black newspapers. Today, only two remain: the *Washington Informer* and the *Afro-American.* Local residents should consciously subscribe to these newspapers, which bring the good and relevant news to the U Street corridor. People can have more than one bank account. One of those accounts should be with the Black-owned bank, Industrial Bank on U Street, which has been supporting the Black Mecca community since 1938. Need flowers and gifts? Go to Lee's Flowers and Card Shop on U Street. Walk the walk of preservation and progress—don't just talk.

No one is saying that change is not good. Change, actually, is the only thing that's permanent. It's here to stay. The good ole days were not so good. But the Black Mecca was. Carter G. Woodson admonished us long ago: "A people who do not know and defend their history and culture is people without a soul. A people with no soul will not be remembered and will be extinguished." As long as they say your name, you remain alive. Let us continue to protect, defend, advocate, advance and celebrate this U Street history and culture and call its name: Be not forgotten, be not denied.

Bernard Demczuk, PhD
Ben's Chili Bowl historian

NOTES

Chapter 1

1. Elizabeth Clark-Lewis, *First Freed: Washington, D.C., in the Emancipation Era* (Washington, D.C.: Howard University Press, 2002), 111.
2. Clinton Yates, "Emancipation Day, D.C.'s Conflicted Holiday," *Washington Post*, April 19, 2013.
3. Clark-Lewis, *First Freed*, 111–12.
4. Constance McLaughlin Green, *The Secret City: History of Race Relations in the Nation's Capital* (Princeton, NJ: Princeton University Press, 1967), 16, 13–14.
5. Maurice Jackson, "Washington, DC: From the Founding of a Slaveholding Capital to a Center of Abolitionism," *Journal of African Diaspora Archaeology & Heritage* 2, no. 1 (2013): 4.
6. McLaughlin Green, *Secret City*, 13–14.
7. Ibid.
8. Jackson, "Washington, DC," 40–41.
9. McLaughlin Green, *Secret City*, 14–15.
10. Jackson, "Washington, DC," 41.
11. McLaughlin Green, *Secret City*, 14.
12. Jackson, "Washington, DC," 41–42.
13. Blair A. Ruble, *Washington's U Street: A Biography* (Baltimore, MD: Johns Hopkins University Press, 2010), 19.
14. Clark-Lewis, *First Freed*, 102.

15. Jackson, "Washington, DC," 42.

16. Patricia Sullivan, "Why Alexandria Lost its D.C." *Washington Post*, October 7, 2011.

17. Jackson, "Washington, DC," 54–55.

18. Mark David Richards, "The Debates over the Retrocession of the District of Columbia, 1801–2004," *Washington History* (Spring/Summer 2004): 71–74, https://www.dcvote.org/sites/default/files/documents/articles/mdrretrocession.pdf.

19. Ibid.

20. "E.S. Abdy Description of a Washington, D.C., Slave Pen," Africans in America, PBS, http://www.pbs.org/wgbh/aia/part4/4h3139t.html.

21. Jackson, "Washington, DC," 44.

22. "E.S. Abdy Description," PBS.

23. "Chapter 8," Charles Dickens, Literature Network, http://www.online-literature.com.

24. Jackson, "Washington, DC," 44.

25. Clark-Lewis, *First Freed*, 75.

26. Jackson, "Washington, DC," 42, 44.

27. McLaughlin Green, *Secret City*,16.

28. Jackson, "Washington, DC," 55.

29. McLaughlin Green, *Secret City*, 17.

30. Pauline Gaskins Mitchell, "The History of Mt. Zion United Methodist Church and Mt. Zion Cemetery," *Records of the Columbia Historical Society, Washington, D.C.* 51 (1984): 103–18, http://www.jstor.org/stable/40067847.

31. McLaughlin Green, *Secret City*, 24–25.

32. "Ending Slavery in the District of Columbia," DC Emancipation Day, DC.gov.

33. Ted Pulliam, "The Dark Days of the Black Codes," Historical Society of the District of Columbia Circuit," http://dcchs.org/Articles/blackcodes.pdf.

34. "Ending Slavery in the District of Columbia," DC Emancipation Day, DC.gov.

35. Ted Pulliam, "The Dark Days of the Black Codes," Historical Society of the District of Columbia Circuit," http://dcchs.org/Articles/blackcodes.pdf.

36. Worthington G. Snethen, *Black Code of the District of Columbia*, New York: William Harned, 1848.

37. Jackson, "Washington, DC," 46.

38. Fred Landon, "Benjamin Lundy in Illinois," *Journal of the Illinois State Historical Society* (1908–1984) 33, no. 1 (1940): 57–67, http://www.jstor.org/stable/40189829.

39. "William Lloyd Garison," Africans in America, PBS, https://www.pbs.org.

40. Benjamin Lundy to Andrew Jackson, September 4, 1823, Andrew Jackson Papers, 1775–1874, Library of Congress, https://www.loc.gov/resource/maj.01063_0397_0399/?sp=1&st=text.

41. "William Lloyd Garison," Africans in America, PBS, https://www.pbs.org/wgbh/aia/part4/4p1561.html.

42. Jackson, "Washington, DC," 46.

43. Megan Specia, "Overlooked No More: How Mary Shadd Cary Shook Up the Abolitionist Movement," *New York Times*, June 6, 2018.

44. Landon, "Benjamin Lundy in Illinois," 57–67.

45. "Freedom's Journal," Black Press, PBS, http://www.pbs.org.

46. Lionel C. Barrow, "We Wish to Plead Our Own Cause: Freedom's Journal the Beginnings of the Black Press," (Annual Meeting of the Association for Education in Journalism, Madison, WI, August 21–24, 1977), https://files.eric.ed.gov/fulltext/ED153236.pdf.

47. "Freedom's Journal," Black Press, PBS, http://www.pbs.org.

48. Jackson, "Washington, DC," 51.

49. Ibid., 53–54.

50. "1820 Missouri Compromise," Compromise of 1850 Heritage Society, http://www.compromise-of-1850.org.

51. "Compromise of 1850," Compromise of 1850 Heritage Society, http://www.compromise-of-1850.org.

52. Jackson, "Washington, DC," 54.

53. "Fugitive Slave Acts," History, February 11, 2020, https://www.history.com.

54. Jackson, "Washington, DC," 54.

55. "Fugitive Slave Acts."

56. Jackson, "Washington, DC," 55.

57. Clark-Lewis, *First Freed*, 73–74.

58. Ibid., 5.

59. Jackson, "Washington, DC," 59.

60. "The Emancipation Proclamation," Online Exhibits, National Archives, https://www.archives.gov.

61. Clark-Lewis, *First Freed*, 80.

62. "Emancipation Proclamation."

63. Jackson, "Washington, DC," 58.
64. Ruble, *Washington's U Street*, 22–25.

Chapter 2

65. Joseph P. Reidy, "Coming from the Shadow of the Past: The Transition from Slavery to Freedom at Freedmen's Village, 1863–1900," *Virginia Magazine of History and Biography* 95, no. 4 (1987): 403–28, http://www.jstor.org/stable/4248971.
66. Michelle Wartman, "Contraband, Runaways, Freemen: New Definitions of Reconstruction Created by the Civil War," International Social Science Review 76, no. 3/4 (2001): 122–29, http://www.jstor.org/stable/41887072.
67. Ruble, *Washington's U Street*, 22.
68. Wartman, "Contraband, Runaways, Freemen," 122–29.
69. Clark-Lewis, *First Freed*, 74.
70. Reidy, "Coming from the Shadow," 403–28.
71. Ruble, *Washington's U Street*, 23.
72. Chris Myers Asch and George Derek Musgrove, *Chocolate City: A History of Race and Democracy in the Nation's Capital* (Chapel Hill: University of North Carolina Press, 2017), 124.
73. Ruble, *Washington's U Street*, 23
74. Asch and Musgrove, *Chocolate City*, 124.
75. Reidy, "Coming from the Shadow," 403–28.
76. Ibid.
77. Ibid.
78. Asch and Musgrove, *Chocolate City*, 124.
79. Reidy, "Coming from the Shadow," 403–28.
80. William J. Wilson, "Letters from 'Ethiop' Number II," Civil War Washington, http://civilwardc.org.
81. Asch and Musgrove, *Chocolate City*, 128.
82. Wilson, "Letters from 'Ethiop' Number II."
83. Asch and Musgrove, *Chocolate City*, 124.
84. "Capitol Hill Facts," Architect of the Capitol, https://www.aoc.gov.
85. Ruble, *Washington's U Street*, 23.
86. Asch and Musgrove, *Chocolate City*, 125.
87. Ibid., 126.
88. Reidy, "Coming from the Shadow," 403–28.

89. Ruble, *Washington's U Street*, 23.

90. Asch and Musgrove, *Chocolate City*, 126.

91. Sharita Thompson (history teacher, Templeton Academy) in discussion with the author, July 2018.

92. Reidy, "Coming from the Shadow," 403–28.

93. Ibid.

94. Ruble, *Washington's U Street*, 23.

95. Asch and Musgrove, *Chocolate City*, 126–28.

96. Ibid., 126.

97. Ruble, *Washington's U Street*, 22–25.

98. Asch and Musgrove, *Chocolate City*, 126–31.

99. Ibid., 137.

100. McLaughlin Green, *Secret City*, 83.

101. Ibid.

102. Ibid.

103. Ibid.

104. Ruble, *Washington's U Street*, 23–24.

105. Asch and Musgrove, *Chocolate City*, 139.

106. McLaughlin Green, *Secret City*, 89.

107. Asch and Musgrove, *Chocolate City*, 139.

108. Gregory Hunter, "Howard University: 'Capstone of Negro Education' During World War II," *Journal of Negro History* 79, no. 1 (1994): 54–70, doi:10.2307/2717667.

109. Asch and Musgrove, *Chocolate City*, 139.

110. Thomas Battle and Clifford Muse, *Howard in Retrospect: Images of the Capstone* (Washington, D.C.: Moorland-Spingarn Research Center, Howard University, 1995).

111. Asch and Musgrove, *Chocolate City*, 139.

112. Battle and Muse, *Howard in Retrospect*.

113. Jimmy Fenison, "Alexander T. Augusta (1825–1890)," BlackPast, March 29, 2009, https://blackpast.org.

114. Ruble, *Washington's U Street*, 23–24.

115. "Dr. Alexander T. Augusta," Howard University, https://150.howard.edu.

116. Casey Nichols, "Kelly Miller (1863–1939)," BlackPast, January 19, 2007, https://blackpast.org.

117. Alonzo Smith, "Howard University," BlackPast, February 8, 2010, http://www.blackpast.org.

118. Gregory, "Howard University," 54–70.

119. Battle and Muse, *Howard in Retrospect*.
120. Ruble, *Washington's U Street*, 107.
121. Asch and Musgrove, *Chocolate City*, 169.
122. Ibid.
123. Ibid., 186.
124. Ibid., 179, 186–87.

Chapter 3

125. "Reconstruction," History, https://www.history.com.
126. Asch and Musgrove, *Chocolate City*, 155; "Alexander Robey Shepherd," Histories of the National Mall, http://mallhistory.org.
127. Ruble, *Washington's U Street*, 27–28.
128. McLaughlin Green, *Secret City*, 97.
129. Robert Harrison, *Washington During Civil War and Reconstruction: Race and Radicalism* (Cambridge: University Press, 2011), 196–98.
130. Ruble, *Washington's U Street*, 31–35.
131. Asch and Musgrove, *Chocolate City*, 155–56.
132. Ibid.
133. Harrison, *Washington During Civil War*, 211.
134. Asch and Musgrove, *Chocolate City*, 156–60.
135. Kate Masur, *An Example for All the Land: Emancipation and the Struggle Over Equality in Washington, D.C.* (Chapel Hill: University of North Carolina Press, 2010), 200.
136. MSRC Staff, "Langson, John Mercer," *Manuscript Division Finding Aids* (2015): 119, https://dh.howard.edu; Asch and Musgrove, *Chocolate City*, 161.
137. Asch and Musgrove, *Chocolate City*, 161–67.
138. Masur, *Example for All the Land*, 214–15.
139. Asch and Musgrove, *Chocolate City*, 163–65.
140. McLaughlin Green, *Secret City*, 113.
141. Asch and Musgrove, *Chocolate City*, 161–67.
142. Ruble, *Washington's U Street*, 34.
143. Asch and Musgrove, *Chocolate City*, 161–67.
144. Ruble, *Washington's U Street*, 34.
145. Asch and Musgrove, *Chocolate City*, 161–67.
146. Ruble, *Washington's U Street*, 35.
147. "Reconstruction."

148. Ruble, *Washington's U Street*, 35.

149. Asch and Musgrove, *Chocolate City*, 161–68.

150. Ruble, *Washington's U Street*, 34–35.

151. Asch and Musgrove, *Chocolate City*, 167–73.

152. Ruble, *Washington's U Street*, 34–35.

153. Asch and Musgrove, *Chocolate City*, 167–73.

154. Ruble, *Washington's U Street*, 49, 51.

155. McLaughlin Green, *Secret City*, 121.

156. Ibid.

157. Ruble, *Washington's U Street*, 35.

158. "The Origins of Jim Crow," Jim Crow Museum of Racist Memorabilia," Ferris State University, https://www.ferris.edu.

159. Ruble, *Washington's U Street*, 49, 51.

160. Asch and Musgrove, *Chocolate City*, 178.

161. McLaughlin Green, *Secret City*, 127.

162. Ruble, *Washington's U Street*, 49–54.

163. "What Was Jim Crow," Jim Crow Museum of Racist Memorabilia, Ferris State University, https://www.ferris.edu.

164. "Plessy v. Ferguson," History, February 21, 2020, https://www.history.com.

165. Ruble, *Washington's U Street*, 51–54.

166. Asch and Musgrove, *Chocolate City*, 179.

167. Ruble, *Washington's U Street*, 55–57.

168. Asch and Musgrove, *Chocolate City*, 179–80.

169. Ruble, *Washington's U Street*, 58–59.

Chapter 4

170. McLaughlin Green, *Secret City*, 155.

171. Ibid., 186.

172. Ibid., 59–60.

173. D.C. Preservation League, *Greater U Street Historic District* (Washington, D.C.: National Park Service, Department of the Interior, 2003), http://dcpreservation-wpengine.netdna-ssl.com/wp-content/uploads/2014/12/U-Street-Brochure.pdf.

174. Asch and Musgrove, *Chocolate City*, 211.

175. Ruble, *Washington's U Street*, 59–60.

176. Ibid., 70.

177. Asch and Musgrove, *Chocolate City*, 210.

178. Michael Andrew Fitzpatrick, "'A Great Agitation for Business': Black Economic Development in Shaw," *Washington History* 2, no. 2 (1990): 48–73, http://www.jstor.org/stable/40073022.

179. Virginia Ali (owner and cofounder of Ben's Chili Bowl), in discussion with the author, November 2016.

180. Elizabeth Clark-Lewis, *Living In, Living Out: African American Domestics in Washington, D.C., 1910–1940* (Washington, D.C.: Smithsonian Books, 2010), preface, 42.

181. Asch and Musgrove, *Chocolate City*, 208.

182. Clark-Lewis, *Living In, Living Out*, 142–72.

183. "Lillian Evanti," White House Historical Association, https://www.whitehousehistory.org.

184. Kathryn S. Smith, "Remembering U Street," *Washington History* 9, no. 2 (1997): 28–53, http://www.jstor.org/stable/40073294.

185. Asch and Musgrove, *Chocolate City*, 206.

186. McLaughlin Green, *Secret City*, 137.

187. Asch and Musgrove, *Chocolate City*, 187, 206.

188. Ibid., 206–7.

189. Eva Wilder McGlasson, "An Earthly Paragon," *Harper's Weekly*, 1892.

190. Asch and Musgrove, *Chocolate City*, 208–10.

191. Fitzpatrick, "A Great Agitation for Business," 53, http://www.jstor.org/stable/40073022.

192. Ibid., 48–73.

193. Smith, "Remembering U Street," 28–53.

194. Ruble, *Washington's U Street*, 70.

195. Asch and Musgrove, *Chocolate City*, 211.

196. Fitzpatrick, "A Great Agitation for Business," 48–73.

197. Ruble, *Washington's U Street*, 65.

198. Smith, "Remembering U Street," 28–53.

199. Maurice Jackson, "Great Black Music and the Desegregation of Washington, D.C.," *Washington History* 26 (2014): 16, http://www.jstor.org/stable/23728366.

200. Ruble, *Washington's U Street*, 66–67.

201. Fitzpatrick, "A Great Agitation for Business," 48–73.

202. Ruble, *Washington's U Street*, 72.

203. John Edward Hasse, "Washington's Duke Ellington," *Washington History* 26 (2014): 39, http://www.jstor.org/stable/23728369.

204. Asch and Musgrove, *Chocolate City*, 212–13.

205. McLaughlin Green, *Secret City*, 168.

206. Ruble, *Washington's U Street*, 66–67.
207. Pero Gaglo Dagbovie, *Carter G. Woodson in Washington D.C.: The Father of Black History* (Charleston, SC: The History Press, 2014), 28.
208. "About NAACP DC Branch," NAACP, http://naacpdc.org.
209. Hasse, "Washington's Duke Ellington," 36–59.

Chapter 5

210. Nancy J. Weiss, "The Negro and the New Freedom: Fighting Wilsonian Segregation," *Political Science Quarterly* 84, no. 1 (1969): 61–79, doi:10.2307/2147047.
211. McLaughlin Green, *Secret City*, 172.
212. "Booker T. Washington," History, December 13, 2019, https://css.history.com.
213. McLaughlin Green, *Secret City*, 163–73.
214. Ibid., 173.
215. Asch and Musgrove, *Chocolate City*, 219–22.
216. Hasse, "Washington's Duke Ellington," 38.
217. Asch and Musgrove, *Chocolate City*, 219–22.
218. Ibid., 223–24.
219. Nancy C. Unger, "Even Judging Woodrow Wilson by the Standards of His Own Time, He Was Deplorably Racist," History News Network, Columbian College of Arts & Sciences, George Washington University, https://historynewsnetwork.org; Nancy C. Unger, *Fighting Bob La Follette* (Madison: Wisconsin Historical Society Press, 2008).
220. Evelyn Brooks-Higginbotham, "The History of Shiloh Baptist Church of Washington, D.C. 1863–1988," Shiloh Baptist Church, http://www.shilohbaptist.org; Asch and Musgrove, *Chocolate City*, 224.
221. "Dr. Booker Taliaferro Washington," Tuskegee University, https://www.tuskegee.edu.
222. "Booker T. Washington and the 'Atlanta Compromise,'" *Defending Freedom, Defining Freedom* (blog), National Museum of African American History & Culture, https://nmaahc.si.edu.
223. "Booker T. Washington's Atlanta Exposition Speech, September 18, 1895," Iowa Department of Cultural Affairs, https://iowaculture.gov.
224. Ruble, *Washington's U Street*, 76–78.
225. McLaughlin Green, *Secret City*, 136.
226. Ibid., 155.

227. Ruble, *Washington's U Street*, 77–78.

228. McLaughlin Green, *Secret City*, 155.

229. "Niagara Movement," History, August 21, 2018, https://www.history.com.

230. "W.E.B. Du Bois," History, December 13, 2019, https://www.history.com.

231. Ruble, *Washington's U Street*, 79.

232. "Introduction," Dr. Kelly Miller: A Resource Guide, Library of Congress, https://www.loc.gov.

233. Herbert Aptheker, "The Washington-Du Bois Conference of 1904," *Science & Society* 13, no. 4 (1949): 344–51, http://www.jstor.org/stable/40399972.

234. Ibid.

235. Ruble, *Washington's U Street*, 80.

236. "Grimké Family Residence Site, African American Heritage Trail," Cultural Tourism DC, https://www.culturaltourismdc.org.

237. Ruble, *Washington's U Street*, 80.

238. Mary Beth Corrigan, "The Emergence of Civil Rights Leaders from the Deep South," Humanities and Social Sciences Online, https://www.h-net.org.

239. Asch and Musgrove, *Chocolate City*, 223.

240. Ruble, *Washington's U Street*, 81.

241. Asch and Musgrove, *Chocolate City*, 224–25.

242. Hamil R. Harris, "39 Year-Old Talks About New Post at Historic D.C. Church," *Washington Post*, June 6, 2014.

243. "Race Discrimination at Washington," *Independent*, November 20, 1913.

244. Asch and Musgrove, *Chocolate City*, 225–26.

245. Ibid., 225–26.

246. Weiss, "Negro and the New Freedom," 61–79.

247. Asch and Musgrove, *Chocolate City*, 226.

248. "World War I," History, https://www.history.com.

249. Asch and Musgrove, *Chocolate City*, 227–28.

250. "Past and Post War," District of Columbia National Guard, https://dc.ng.mil.

251. Asch and Musgrove, *Chocolate City*, 227–28.

252. Ruble, *Washington's U Street*, 83.

253. Archibald Grimké, "The Shame of America," in *Freedom on My Mind*, ed. Manning Marable (New York: Columbia University Press, 2003), 543.

254. Asch and Musgrove, *Chocolate City*, 232.

255. Peter Perl, "Nation's Capital Held at Mercy of the Mob," *Washington Post*, July 16, 1989.
256. Asch and Musgrove, *Chocolate City*, 232–35; Ruble, *Washington's U Street*, 83–86; Perl, "Nation's Capital."
257. Asch and Musgrove, *Chocolate City*, 234.

Chapter 6

258. Richard Lee (second-generation owner of Lee's Flower and Card Shop), in discussion with the author, October 2016.
259. Ruble, *Washington's U Street*, 165.
260. Teresa Wiltz, "U Turn the Fabled D.C. Street That Played Host to Duke Ellington and Pearl Bailey Reinvents Itself Once More," *Washington Post*, March 5, 2006.
261. Asch and Musgrove, *Chocolate City*, 238–39.
262. Maurice Jackson and Blair A. Ruble, eds. *DC Jazz: Stories of Jazz Music in Washington, DC* (Washington, D.C.: Georgetown University Press, 2018), 39.
263. Representative Eleanor Holmes Norton (District of Columbia representative), in discussion with the author, March 2019.
264. Sandra Fitzpatrick and Maria R. Goodwin, *The Guide to Black Washington: Places and Events of Historical and Cultural Significance in the Nation's Capital* (New York: Hipocrene Books, 1999), 75.
265. Kenneth Alphonso Mitchell, "The Story of Dunbar High School: How Students from the First Public High School for Black Students in the United States Influenced America" (Master's thesis, Georgetown University, 2012), https://repository.library.georgetown.edu; "Dunbar HS History," Dunbar Alumni Federation, http://daf-dc.org; Sandra Fitzpatrick and Maria R. Goodwin, "Shaw West: A Walking Tour," in *The Guide to Black Washington: Places and Events of Historical and Cultural Significance in the Nation's Capital* (New York: Hippocrene Books, 2001), 156.
266. Ruble, *Washington's U Street*, 164.
267. Ibid., 111–14.
268 Kevin Hart (pastor of the Christian Tabernacle Church), in discussion with the author, February 2019.
269. Fitzpatrick and Goodwin, "Shaw West," 156.
270. "History," St. Luke's Episcopal Church, http://stlukesdc.org.
271. Fitzpatrick and Goodwin, "Shaw West," 128.

272. Vermont Avenue Baptist Church, http://www.vabc.org.

273. Dr. Judith A. Webb (historian for the Historic Phyllis Wheatley YWCA), in discussion with the author, May 2019.

274. Richard I. McKinney, "Mordecai Johnson: An Early Pillar of African-American Higher Education," *Journal of Blacks in Higher Education* no. 27 (2000): 99–104. doi:10.2307/2679021.

275. Ruble, *Washington's U Street*, 156.

276. "True Reformer Building History," Public Welfare Foundation, https://www.publicwelfare.org; Fitzpatrick and Goodwin, "Shaw West," 168–69.

277. "History of Washington D.C. YMCA," YMCA of Metropolitan Washington, https://www.ymcadc.org; "The USO Mission: Serving the Troops for 71 Years," USO, February 4, 2012, https://www.uso.org.

278. "Anthony Bowen History," YMCA of Metropolitan Washington, https://www.ymcadc.org.

279. B. Doyle Mitchell Jr. (president and CEO of Industrial Bank), in discussion with the author, November 2016.

280. "Industrial Bank of Washington, African American Heritage Trail," Cultural Tourism DC, https://www.culturaltourismdc.org.

281. Richard Lee and Stacie Lee Banks (chairman of the board and president of Lee's Flower and Card Shop), in discussion with the author, October 2016.

282. "Whitelaw Apartment House, 1839 Thirteenth Street Northwest, Washington, District of Columbia, DC," https://www.loc.gov/item/dc0299/.

283. Virginia Ali (owner and cofounder of Ben's Chili Bowl), in discussion with the author, November 2016.

284. Ruble, *Washington's U Street*, 116–18; Asch and Musgrove, *Chocolate City*, 261–62; Mary-Elizabeth B. Murphy, *Jim Crow Capital: Women and Black Freedom Struggles in Washington, D.C., 1920–1945* (Chapel Hill: University of North Carolina Press, 2018), 125–26.

285. Gretchen Wharton (D.C. native and lifelong Shaw community resident and activist), in discussion with the author, October 2019.

286. Fitzpatrick and Goodwin, "Shaw West," 122–23.

287. Carol M. Highsmith, photographer, "Stairway at the Restored Lincoln Theatre, Washington, D.C. United States Washington D.C.," between 1980 and 2006, photograph, https://www.loc.gov/item/2011636444.

288. Fitzpatrick and Goodwin, "Shaw West," 171.

289. Jackson and Ruble, *DC Jazz*, 51.

290. Fitzpatrick and Goodwin, "Shaw West," 143.

291. Ibid., 166–67; Jackson and Ruble, *DC Jazz*, 39–40.
292. Ruble, *Washington's U Street*, 148–50.

Chapter 7

293. Ibid., 120–21, 123.
294. Ibid.,159.
295. Asch and Musgrove, *Chocolate City*, 273.
296. Langston Hughes and Christopher C. De Santis, *The Collected Works: Fight for Freedom and Other Writings on Civil Rights* (Columbia: University of Missouri Press, 2001), 94.
297. Asch and Musgrove, *Chocolate City*, 273.
298. Howard Brick, "The Other March on Washington," *Jacobin*, https://www.jacobinmag.com.
299. Jennifer Scanlon, *Until There Is Justice: The Life of Anna Arnold Hedgeman* (New York: Oxford University Press US, 2019), 92; "Brotherhood of Sleeping Car Porters," VCU Libraries Social Welfare History Project, https://socialwelfare.library.vcu.edu.
300. "Nation's Premier Civil Rights Organization," NAACP, https://www.naacp.org.
301. Ruble, *Washington's U Street*, 120–21, 122.
302. Hughes and De Santis, *Collected Works*, 93–94.
303. "A. Philip Randolph," AFL-CIO, https://aflcio.org.
304. Erik Gellman, "When Fighting Racism Meant Fighting Economic Exploitation," interview by Shawn Gude, *Jacobin*, https://www.jacobinmag.com.
305. Asch and Musgrove, *Chocolate City*, 266–68.
306. Hughes and De Santis, *Collected Works*, 93–95.
307. Howard Brick and Christopher Phelps, *Radicals in America: The U.S. Left Since the Second World War* (New York: Cambridge University Press, 2016), 3.
308. Ruble, *Washington's U Street*, 104.
309. W.E.B. Du Bois, "The Taented Tenth," Teaching American History, https://teachingamericanhistory.org.
310. Gary M. Lavergne, *Before Brown: Heman Marion Sweatt, Thurgood Marshall, and the Long Road to Justice* (Austin: University of Texas Press, 2010), 34.
311. Ibid., 35.
312. Ibid.

313. "NAACP History: Charles Hamilton Houston," NAACP, https://www.naacp.org.
314. "About Charles Hamilton Houston," Amherst College, https://www.amherst.edu.
315. "NAACP History: Charles Hamilton Houston."
316. "Charles Hamilton Houston: A Gallery," Legal Information Institute, Cornell Law School, https://www.law.cornell.edu.
317. Ruble, *Washington's U Street*, 98–100.
318. "Our History," Howard University School of Law, http://law.howard.edu.
319. Gary M. Lavergne, *Before Brown: Heman Marion Sweatt, Thurgood Marshall, and the Long Road to Justice* (Austin: University of Texas Press, 2010), 34.
320. Ruble, *Washington's U Street*, 102.
321. Ibid., 102–3.
322. Asch and Musgrove, *Chocolate City*, 287–88.
323. Charles H. Houston, "The Need for Negro Lawyers," *Journal of Negro Education* 4, no. 1 (1935): 49–52, doi:10.2307/2292085.
324. Ibid.
325. Larry S. Gibson, *Young Thurgood: The Making of a Supreme Court Justice* (Amherst, NY: Prometheus Books, 2012), 41–45, 107–12.
326. Ruble, *Washington's U Street*, 97.
327. "William Henry Hastie (1904–1976)," Brown at 50, Howard University School of Law, http://law.howard.edu.
328. "James Nabrit Jr.," National Park Service, https://www.nps.gov.
329. William Glaberson, "A. Leon Higginbotham Jr., Federal Judge, Is Dead at 70," *New York Times*, December 15, 1998; "Charles Hamilton Houston (1895–1950)," Brown at 50, Howard University School of Law, http://law.howard.edu.
330. "Thurgood Marshall 1940–1961," Legal Defense and Educational Fund, https://www.naacpldf.org.
331. Ruble, *Washington's U Street*, 103.
332. Ibid., 117–19.
333. Asch and Musgrove, *Chocolate City*, 280–83.
334. Ruble, *Washington's U Street*, 104.
335. J. Samuel Walker, *Most of 14ᵗʰ Street Is Gone: The Washington, DC Riots of 1968* (New York: Oxford University Press, 2018), 16.
336. MSRC Staff, *Consolidated Parent Group Inc* (Washington, D.C.: Manuscript Division Finding Aids, 2015); Ruble, *Washington's U Street*, 105–6; Asch and Musgrove, *Chocolate City*, 304–7.

337. Debra Michals, "Ruby Bridges," National Women's History Museum, https://www.womenshistory.org.

338. "D.C. Home Rule," Council of the District of Columbia, https://dccouncil.us.

339. "Civil Rights Movement," History, June 23, 2020, https://www.history.com.

340. Richard I. McKinney, "Mordecai Johnson: An Early Pillar of African-American Higher Education," *Journal of Blacks in Higher Education*, no. 27 (2000): 99–104, doi:10.2307/2679021.

341. Ruble, *Washington's U Street*, 201.

342. Walker, *Most of 14th Street*, 25–27.

Chapter 8

343. Ruble, *Washington's U Street*, 300.

344. Ibid., 202.

345. Kenneth Carroll, "The Meanings of Funk," *Washington Post*, February 1, 1998.

346. Ruble, *Washington's U Street*, 261.

347. Marc Fisher, "Rapture in the Streets as Multitudes Cheer Obama and Celebrate America," *Washington Post*, November 6, 2008.

348. Marissa J. Lang, "'Where's My Go-Go Music?' Residents Say Turn Up the Music After a Complaint Silenced a D.C. Intersection," *Washington Post*, April 9, 2019.

349. Ruble, *Washington's U Street*, 206.

350. "Washington D.C. Region," University of Minnesota Law, https://www.law.umn.edu.

351. Darren Jones (Ward 1 native and president of Pleasant Plains Civic Association), in discussion with the author, May 2019.

352. "Mapping Neighborhood Change & Gentrification in Southern California County," Urban Displacement Project, https://www.urbandisplacement.org.

353. Sarah Meehan, "Baltimore Among Nation's Most Gentrified Cities, Study Shows," *Baltimore Sun*, March 20, 2019.

354. "D.C. Home Rule," Council of the District of Columbia; "Advisory Neighborhood Commissions," DC Gov, https://anc.dc.gov.

355. "Mayors of the District of Columbia Since Home Rule."

356. "Advisory Neighborhood Commissions."

357. Darren Jones discussion with the author.

358. Walker, *Most of 14ᵗʰ Street*, 25.

359. Ibid., 49–60.

360. Ruble, *Washington's U Street*, 214–17.

361. Ernie Jarvis (fifth generation Washingtonian, grandson of Dr. Charles Drew and son of former D.C. councilmember Charlene Drew Jarvis), in discussion with the author, April 2020.

362. Asch and Musgrove, *Chocolate City*, 382.

363. Carroll, "Meanings of Funk."

364. Carroll, "Meanings of Funk"; Sara R. Gregg, "A Teen-Agers' D.C. Is Filled with Go-Go," *Washington Post*, August 23, 1982; John Kelly, "A New Apartment Building on Eighth Street NW Is Named for Jim Shay, a D.C. Original," *Washington Post*, March 29, 2014.

365. Jarvis in discussion with the author.

366. "Washington in the 2000s," PBS, https://www.pbs.org.

367. "QuickFacts District of Columbia," United States Census Bureau, https://www.census.gov.

368. Wharton in discussion with the author.

369. Derek Hyra, *Race, Class, and Politics in the Cappuccino City* (Chicago: University of Chicago Press, 2017), 3–6.

370. Steve Hendrix, "In a Changing D.C., Martha's Table Plans a $20 Million Move to Southeast," *Washington Post*, May 4, 2015.

371. Anthony Williams (D.C. mayor from 1999 to 2007), in discussion with the author, June 2019.

372. Asch and Musgrove, *Chocolate City*, 341–42.

373. Ruble, *Washington's U Street*, 228–38.

374. Wanda Henderson (U Street business owner and Ledroit Park native), in discussion with the author, April 2020.

375. Briana Thomas, "Community Leaders Push to Make Go-Go the Official Music of D.C.," *Afro*, November 7, 2019.

376. Stephanie Barbara Frank, "'If We Own the Story, We Own the Place': Cultural Heritage, Historic Preservation, and Gentrification on U Street" (master's thesis, University of Maryland, 2005), https://drum.lib.umd.edu.

INDEX

ABOUT THE AUTHOR

Briana A. Thomas spotlights the Black history of U Street in her debut book with a compilation of community storytelling, memory-jogging artifacts and thoughtful memorabilia. Briana has been published in *Washingtonian Magazine*, the historic *Afro-American* newspaper and the *Washington Post* throughout her journalism career. Briana earned a master's of journalism from the University of Maryland–College Park and a bachelor of arts in English and communications from Greensboro College. Briana is the co-pastor of a Maryland-based multisite church, Open Bible Ministries.